Buying to Rent

Buying to Rent

The Key to Your Financial Freedom

Nick Rampley-Sturgeon

FT Prentice Hall
FINANCIAL TIMES

An imprint of **Pearson Education**

PEARSON EDUCATION LIMITED

Edinburgh Gate
Harlow, Essex CM20 2JE
Tel: +44 (0)1279 623623
Fax: +44 (0)1279 431059
Website: www.pearson.com

First published in Great Britain in 2002

ISBN: 0 273 66109 4

British Library Cataloguing in Publication Data
A catalogue record for this book can be obtained from the British Library

10 9 8

Typeset by Land & Unwin (Data Sciences) Ltd, Northampton
Printed and bound in Great Britain by Biddles Ltd, King's Lynn, Norfolk

The Publishers' policy is to use paper manufactured from sustainable forests.

Contents

Acknowledgements

With grateful thanks to the many individuals who showed kindness and great patience in sharing with me details of the way they run their businesses. With every question they showed enthusiasm for the project and demonstrated great wisdom and insight.

In particular, I would like to thank Paul and Sarah of Murray Properties; Paul Gregson of Knight Frank for the Caribbean; David Vaughn of Sotogrande in Spain; Simon Malster of French Ski Property; Phillipe Pièdon-Lavaux (Notaire Stagiaire) of Blake Lapthorn Solicitors; Sylvia Stimson from Derbyshire Country Cottages for her valuable help and support on working with the UK holiday market; and Steven Sykes of Sands Property Search for his time and wisdom in respect of the auction process.

Special thanks to John and Barbara Moseley for giving me the time and space at Jubilee Cottage to write the book.

To my wife Joanna, for handling all the 'stuff' of everyday life so brilliantly while this book was being written. Above all to our boys – Henry and Johnny – for teaching us the importance of creating a legacy through property investment – and for asking me if *Buying to Rent* will be as good as *Tintin* and *Red Rackham's Treasure*. I hope so!

Introduction

I bet that at some point in recent times you will have uttered words to the effect of: 'If only I had another house that I could rent out.'

You may have said this quietly to yourself, or discussed it with your partner. Perhaps you even had a heated discussion on the topic with friends one night over a few drinks. What I am certain of is that you have been held back by what you see as difficult circumstances, uncertain financial markets, apparent lack of income, or not knowing where to start.

This book has been written to help you understand some simple principles of residential property investment so that you can enjoy the peace of mind that comes from being able to supplement your job or work income with an extra property that gives you a rental income. You might choose to use the increased knowledge you gain on this topic to buy more than one extra home, developing a portfolio of revenue streams that will benefit your lifestyle. There are also some tax advantages involved in not depending solely on a boss or an employer for your household income each month.

If you could match your current income from the rental of another property or perhaps from a couple of properties and effectively double your income, what would you do with it? Would you keep the job and continue to invest? Would you consider a part-time opportunity with your work while developing further income? Whatever your first thoughts are, the key is that owning a property gives you *choice*. With the option to choose comes the benefit of knowing that you can take back control of your financial future and release your sole dependency on the work place for your money.

Years ago I realised that some people had things in life which others appeared to have no chance of achieving. While some groups of people were able to live a more relaxed lifestyle where they could enjoy a few or even a lot of extras, there were larger groups of people barely making it and setting their sums back to zero at the start of each month.

As a student I began to see the futility of paying out rent each month, whether it was for a bedsit or for my share of a terraced house I rented with friends. I frequently had late night conversations with my fellow students about how much rent we would hand over to landlords during the course of our degrees. As I moved further through my degree, I began to see the successes of students who had graduated and still lived within a few miles of the college. Those who lived and worked nearby, and who had invested since graduating in one or perhaps two houses for rental were far more sure of their future than the ones who were working to cover house bills from their own wages or salaries.

I finally clicked on the biggest single difference between the aforementioned two groups of people. The relaxed group of people who took a more confident view, who seemed to know they would be financially sound even if there were a downturn in the economy or if they experienced ill-health, these were the people and families who owned at least one other property aside from the one they lived in.

So many other students said the same as me: 'When we graduate let's buy a house back here and rent it out.' Yet of all the people I have kept in touch with since those days, none of them ever made that investment in a house for renting out to other people. Why not? Had they forgotten our conversations? I doubt it. They had simply started work and found themselves working for an income and then discovered that they needed all that money simply to survive.

> **What about you? Have you sat around that table with friends and talked about the perfect sense in getting a rental property?**

What about you? Have you sat around that table with friends and talked about the perfect sense in getting a rental property? Have you chatted with someone as you walked across a field after a great pub lunch on a sunny afternoon about how great it would be to be able to take more time off work to do things just like this. If only there was a way that you could afford to do so. There is a better way. This is it.

I am not a full-time property investor even though our property investments give us an income to enjoy, and this is not a book about becoming a multi-millionaire overnight. However, it is realistic to use the principles and tips within this book to help yourself towards a secure financial independence based on developing a portfolio of rented properties. I'm aiming to give you enough knowledge and confidence to act on the information in this book and to discover for yourself how you can move forward financially through having at least one rented property aside from the place where you live yourself.

Consider this. If you had as much disposable money coming in each month to represent approximately the equivalent of a week's salary, would you notice the difference? Of course you would. Yet how easy is it for you to get a 25 per cent pay rise? What would be required of you to get this type of promotion, and how likely is it to happen?

In the years since I rented out my first house it has consistently brought in a gross rent roughly equivalent to a quarter of my net income from work. After the allowable expenses of maintaining the property each year our return on investment has provided sufficient income to pay for our annual holidays, or to provide for our son's education, or to bring in enough to buy a second home overseas, or the equivalent to what it costs us to run two cars each year. The income from just that first house, rented out effectively, gives us a lot of comfort and protection against the outside world. Imagine the strength and confidence that having three or four separate properties can bring to you and your family. It is this independence I want to share through this book, just as we do with our Property Bootcamp events.

> The benefits of receiving rental income have been valuable and often most timely, especially when my income as a self-employed worker dipped or was slow coming in.

I first got into rental property almost by accident when I bought a house with a friend who then moved to a company in a new location. Rather than lose out financially, I bought his half back from him, rented out first one bedroom, then a second, before finally moving out myself and renting the whole house to tenants. The benefits of receiving rental income have been valuable and often most timely, especially when my income as a self-employed worker dipped or was slow coming in.

Have I said enough to convince you of the merits of Buying to Rent? Remember that beyond the additional cashflow from rent there lies a further benefit. This is the lump sum of cash that comes from selling a property occasionally or regularly as the property appreciates in value and you choose to access the equity. What you do with these bonuses is another matter and I hope you have fun with this extra growth in property value too.

Enjoy the book and the application of the tips and ideas contained within. Learn from the real-life stories of how other people have approached the subject from their own unique circumstances. You can soon be enjoying an extra income because you have seen the sense of Buying to Rent. I know you can.

Nick Rampley-Sturgeon
Runswick Bay

The situation and the opportunity

The situation

> We all get seduced by the promise of a regular income, a nice annual bonus, or perhaps the safety and security of working with a long-established company.

Events in the United States in September 2001 have caused people to look again at the issue of work-life balance. Fear brought about by the tragedies has seen a rise in the cost of rural and secluded property in out-of-the-way areas. We all want to feel a little more secure and less vulnerable.

As this book was going to final draft several global giants in the motor industry announced profit falls and the loss of tens of thousands of jobs, and telecommunications companies have spent many months shedding staff in the light of the reducing demand for their personal mobile phones. At a local level we all know people affected by redundancy, shrinkage, downsizing and rationalisation. Fewer companies are expecting to take on a surplus of new people over and above the numbers who leave. We all see people who are up there riding the corporate gravy train one day, only to appear the next moment as the victim of a corporate process of 'letting-go'.

So much of who we believe ourselves to be is tied in with the roles we have and the jobs we perform that when the job is gone, all of a sudden we question who we are. The saddest thing is that people are often not in control of their finances when this happens. We all get seduced by the promise of a regular income, a nice annual bonus, or perhaps the safety and security of working with a long-established company or a good local government organisation.

The reason we identify so easily with people who lose their livelihoods as they lose their jobs, is that we know too well the fear that is expressed in the phrase 'there but for the Grace of God, go I'. For most of the working population there is a deep-down and little-talked-about fear of being less than three months away from personal insolvency. Just going

12 weeks without our income would reduce most of us to a dreadful state, unable to pay the bills and increasingly moving towards a situation where it would be difficult to borrow for the short-term in the hope that we could turn things around and find more work.

Safe investments?

As I write this, household net worth has been falling at its fastest rate for more than two years, eroded by the falling stock market and further battered by the decline or even the collapse of pension fund providers. Within Britain, where many people see their home and its valuation as an indication of their net worth, people seem to be looking nervously at the economy at the same time that they are regarding their own regular income and personal finances with some nervousness.

The inability of the national state pension in Britain to keep pace with inflation, and particularly with the fast-rising cost of living, is forcing more people to look elsewhere for security. Company pension provision may be an aspect of full-time employment but the results produced by pension companies have been poor to average in most instances.

Beyond this, the ability of a pension to pay out at your retirement age is being decimated by the smaller number of contributors to the fund as people become less willing to commit to such long-term savings for such a poor guarantee of return in their later years. This distrust of financial services has, of course, been heightened by corporate scandals like those of Maxwell and, more recently, the US power company Enron.

For example, one Enron employee had contributed heavily to shares in the company, assuming they were protected. Aged 63 he had amassed savings of $740 000 in a pension plan and expected this would give him a comfortable regular dividend for his retired years. After the fiasco, his holdings in shares other than Enron are worth just $10 000 and he will now have to keep working until he is 69 to build up a few more thousand dollars before he will be forced to retire. Of course, his holding was unusual in that it was not a diversified spread, yet, regardless of this, he had assumed that regulatory and audit bodies would have protected his interests. In the event that you have a variety of savings already, how sure can you be that they are being looked after wisely, or that the companies and businesses you have chosen to invest with are being adequately overseen by regulators?

Back in the UK, new rises in council tax are likely to be announced if plans are approved by the government. Homes in Britain valued for assessment purposes at 1993 figures are likely to be re-valued and charged for rates at a more recent valuation figure, again putting pressure on each household to find this extra income.

The increasing longevity of people is yet another reason for you to look at stable ways of investing for the years after 50 when the opportunities for leisure and travel are there, but the money often is absent.

By looking at ways of developing other income alongside our jobs and professions it is possible to recover our sense of personal control, while at the same time creating the possibility that we might then be able to choose a life more suited to who we really want to be.

The opportunity

Where do you figure in all these trends? Do you feel that your job is secure or are you feeling under pressure?

My wife and I have been self-employed since the early 1990s and in this time have noticed an increase in the number of people who talk freely about their worries and concerns about financial security. Where it was once rare to have a stranger open up about the issues that trouble them or to hear from a family at the school gates about money challenges, it seems that the world is more open on these topics nowadays.

> By looking at ways of developing other income alongside our jobs and professions it is possible to recover our sense of personal control.

With this greater freedom of discussion of the effect of the economy and politics upon our personal finances has come the debate about how we survive our current and future years. This is why people are increasingly looking at property as a route to generating current income and future assets.

Here is your opportunity

Below are some examples of the ways that people are turning to property investment to create the security that they have been unable to find elsewhere. These and other examples will be explored further within the book, but look to see what appeals to you and use them to prompt thinking about your own situation. Think about your own circumstances right now and of your reaction to these simplified stories about what others have done and how they achieved their goals through their purchase of property assets.

Outcome: Barry and Lou

A couple in their early thirties have just moved into their 200-year-old dream home on several acres of land with a small fishing lake in the north of England. They did this just three years after starting to buy up terraced houses which needed decorating before reletting them to tenants. They collect the rent themselves rather than use an agency.

Their original vision   For several years after they first met they talked with us whenever we got together about the circumstances they wanted to create for their children, and had identified that this was likely to be financed by a few rented houses. Barry worked then as a jobbing builder and wanted to create an income that would be constant even if he were injured and unable to work.

Outcome: Ben

A single man in south-east England has three houses on the coast that he rents out and is looking for a second flat in central London. He sees that two more properties will allow him to give up the day job and the un-pleasant commute to spend more time working as a freelancer from home.

His original vision   Ben has worked in a job that he does not totally enjoy for several years. However, he saw this as necessary for raising the finance that would allow him to buy a rented property. The real goal was always to be self-employed as a personal development coach; able to focus on the quality of the work he did rather than on how much work he generated from his clients.

Outcome: Nicola

A single woman is confidently approaching the task of buying a large property and subdividing it into three living units that she will rent to tenants. On the cash-flow figures agreed with her bank she is going to purchase a second house for herself.

Her original vision   When we first spoke she expressed how she felt financially trapped by her earnings that would not allow her a step on the property ladder. As a single person she felt that she had a lower standard of living than married friends where two incomes were paying for a mortgage. She was keen to move out of her small flat and create more space for herself.

Outcome: John and Charlotte

A couple who love the countryside have purchased a three-bedroom cottage in a small market town and have put it in the hands of a specialist holiday lettings company. They will have use of the property and its views across beautiful scenery for 20 weeks of the year; the rest of the time it is let out in either weekend or week-long lets. They have a delightful holiday home that will be paid for by the holiday lettings.

Their original vision   Faced with retirement in 10 years, they both wanted to be able to spend more time in their favourite part of the country. Knowing that property in the region is much sought-after, they chose to buy early and opted for a house that would provide them with several positive choices when they reached retirement. They looked at properties in a popular location before settling on one where the income from holiday lettings was twice the value of their annual mortgage and maintenance payments.

Outcome: Michael

A 23-year-old from a regional city works in an office and earns just an average wage for the area, yet he owns four terraced houses and a rent roll each month that exceeds his job income. He is continuing to reinvest the majority of his rental income and looking for further properties.

His original vision   Aware of the financial hardships experienced by some of the friends who left school at the same time, he opted to be less dependent upon his job and always to be protected by rental income.

Outcome: Graeme and Jo

At a recent auction a couple who are new to investing in property acquired a two-bedroom terraced house which rents out at £260 per month. They bought the house for just £5600. After some decoration the house has already been valued at three times the purchase price.

Their original vision   Working in an area away from their main home, he researched local property prices and the publicised impending development of an inner-city community area. From looking for repossession properties at auction, they identified that this would be a route to create regular income alongside the uncertainty of his job.

Outcome: Frank and Candy

A trainer and his wife run a business together that involves him travelling extensively around Europe. With some of his earnings they have invested in a villa on the Mediterranean coast of Spain. Before the construction has finished they already have bookings for ten weeks of rental each year.

Their original vision   Having a base in Southern Europe would allow them to bid with some legitimacy for Spanish and French business and to travel easily between contracts. They narrowed the search to several towns with marinas and close to good regional airports.

Each of the seven individuals or families whose story is outlined briefly above had a strategy for investing and there was a clear goal and vision they were seeking to achieve. Take a few moments now to look at this approach, because you can create the outcome you want for yourself if you can first picture it *before* you go and buy the property investment.

What are you seeking?

Do you expect that the money you generate will solve all your problems? Are you imagining there to be a certain amount of money that, once you have set it up as a monthly rent roll, will be all you need for ever?

How about education for your children? Have you considered what the cost of education will be 17 years from now for a child who is now just a year old, and who will want to complete a four-year degree course? If the cost of living almost doubles every seven years and the value of money falls due to the cost of living, then how much do you need to be putting aside right now from the small amount that you have left over each month? Hardly inspiring is it?

How about the cost of clearing the debt on your combined car loans or even your car and any personal loans you still have outstanding? If you could pay these off in half of the existing term of repayment is it likely that you could motivate yourself to see the value in creating something. In the event that you suffer a long-term debilitating illness that prevents you from being able to work, how long would you last on the savings you have right now? Three months? Six months? Use Fig. 1.1 to help you list events that may threaten your lifestyle.

And what about the positive benefits of being able to create an income that you can enjoy in the present while you have the ability to travel or lead a busy life? While the pointers raised before were largely about

Figure 1.1

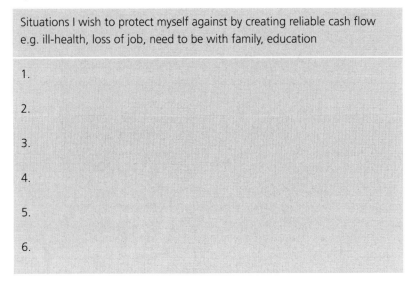

Situations I wish to protect myself against by creating reliable cash flow
e.g. ill-health, loss of job, need to be with family, education

1.

2.

3.

4.

5.

6.

planning for the future, it is just as important to see that what you do
with property and the creation of an income-producing asset in the present.
It might take some work to invest in two or three rental properties, yet the
benefit in terms of a steady cash flow would be enormous to you and to
the wish list you identify for yourself with Fig. 1.2.

Figure 1.2

Goals I would like to accomplish based on regular additional cash flow
e.g. more travel, the opportunity to return to education, the ability to live
in a location we choose and not be dependent upon a job

1.

2.

3.

4.

5.

6.

Why this book?

I n coming to look at the topic of renting and how I came to be a landlord, it was inevitable I should look at the routes I took to gain an understanding of money and its function in my own life. The more I began to research my own experience of money, the more I realised that I couldn't separate this from what I had been taught about money – deliberately or otherwise – while I was growing up. My money history could not be separated from the story of my childhood.

My money history

I grew up in the centre of a pleasant village surrounded by a community. My father worked in the construction industry as a quantity surveyor while my mother had been a teacher and then stayed at home to look after us. We went to the local schools, had regular holidays at the seaside and at weekends spent lots of time walking in the national parks.

Even when I was at school I could see that some children's parents worked for a company while another child's parents owned the company; that one family struggled to afford an annual holiday while another family flew overseas for two or three great trips each year. Why did some kids live in different houses, attend different schools and have different clothes? How come some children worked for pocket money and others were given it by their parents? I noticed different patterns of behaviour among people and families when it came to money and the experiences of these groups were diverse. I learned a lot by observing them and the way they led their lives, as outlined in these examples.

The self-employed family

Uncle Bob Uncle Bob was my mother's older brother and ran a furniture business with a small number of shops established by my grandfather. Uncle Bob's family's big modern house was very different from ours, individually designed by an architect and in a great location next to other fascinating houses. He always seemed to be happy and loud and having fun. While this was part of his character and personality, I can also see that he was an entrepreneur and enjoyed being so. His owning a business attracted me even from the age of five or six.

I was always aware that this was very different from my father's job with a company. My father worked long hours and never really spoke of his job, other than to describe the constant wrangling that went on between him, his company and contractors on building projects. I don't think my parents ever considered self-employment or explored the benefits of owning a successful business.

> I don't think my parents ever considered self-employment or explored the benefits of owning a successful business.

Uncle Philip and Aunty Mary They ran two factories producing leather goods and ceramic ware and employed what seemed like loads of staff. They were strong on the work ethic and determined to gain benefits for their family while being good to their staff.

The property-owning families

The developers Another business-owning family that fascinated me worked as property developers, focusing on commercial buildings and offices. Their grown-up children obviously understood their parents' business and seemed to accept and take for granted that they should enjoy looking to the future with confidence and a degree of certainty given the assets that had been created and built up over years by their parents.

Nigel and the chip shops Nigel was a classmate at secondary school and came from the same village as me. His father had half a dozen fish and chip shops in the local town, all in areas where take-out food was a tradition and where rents and the labour costs of operating his shops were low. Nigel's pocket money was the considerable profits on the fruit and games machines in the shops, but it was his job as he got older to clean them, empty them and maintain them. What really struck me about this business though, was that the real hidden asset of the business was not the strong cash flow of money being handed over the counter for bags of chips. His customers were paying his mortgages.

The long-term investor

When I was in my teens a man who was to have a profound impact on my thinking moved into the village. His name was Henry and he was a retired man who had worked as an accountant in Latin America in the 1930s and then lived in the Channel Islands before their seizure by the Germans. I loved his stories and tales of adventure but he also often spoke to me about the value of investing and the need to set aside funds for an enjoyable retirement. To a boy of perhaps 14 this seemed like an eternity away and much of what he shared was above my understanding, but I knew that he was teaching me pointers and principles of investing that I had never heard about at home and which had never been mentioned at school.

The point of telling you about these families or individuals is that they were the financial role models that I had as a child, the people who actually took the time to explain their business or their interests so that I could understand them. For them, the topic of money was as interesting and fascinating as any other aspect of life. Clearly, several of them attributed great importance to its understanding and its teaching.

Within our own home money was never discussed in a way that I can remember and to this day I don't know what my parents have ever earned or what they receive as pensions. It is simply not a subject for discussion.

Here's the real point. Not talking about money is common in families and the reasons are as broad as they are deep. When I consider the financial issues that we as children have had to work through on our own, I have to wonder whether the same challenges would have come up if money had been a topic to be discussed during childhood. Every one of us has struggled to come to terms with wages, credit cards, housing rent and eventually mortgages. Might I have coped with my credit card problems at university better? Might I have thought differently about relying on an overdraft if I had been shown that I could be making my own money by being in business for myself?

Whatever the answer to those particular questions we all have 'stuff' about money in our heads. By discussion with friends and colleagues and listening to their stories about money issues, it seems rare for families to have done much to help their children develop an understanding of money that is interesting and wholesome, let alone one that produces a legacy of value. If we are lucky, someone will take us by the hand and tell us a little about how money works in the world. If we are unlucky, we can end up going through some terrible learning on our own and this can be financially as well as emotionally very painful!

Yet the experience and the discussion never ends. Every week I speak to individuals or to groups who are keen to get a better handle on their circumstances financially. They have done some good things or they have not. They have some money or they have none. They are tenants of landlords or they are landlords looking for a sense of direction. This book is intended to help you regardless of your circumstances and in spite of your financial situation.

Exploring your family history

In your own experience you will have been given lessons about money and its function in life. From the first day that you received pocket money or an allowance, to the point where you are now and earning a salary or a regular wage, you have been constantly making decisions about money and its meaning and purpose for you.

People who are self-employed frequently tell me of a link or a pattern that they can see in their own circumstances. It is common for them to speak of a sense of not being in control when they were young children and resolving to be in control one day. Even though this has led to opting for the self-employed way of life, such a choice does not mean that all self-employed people have a tight handle on finance. Far from it! It just means that they grew up with as much confusion about money as the next person!

Some questions you might consider are:

■ What assumptions have you made about money that came from your childhood?

■ Can you remember who your role models were about money?

■ What about the people who taught you about money in a negative or neutral sense?

■ Think of a situation or a turning point that has helped you to see money in a useful light.

■ Did you receive pocket money as a child? Did you have to do anything for it?

■ Were you ever asked to account for the pocket money in terms of how you spent it or saved it?

I ask that last question because as children when we received money there was usually no need to account for it. I am convinced of the link between easy pocket money and the easy spending habits of adults with credit cards, not required to account for whether they spent it on something

Figure 2.1

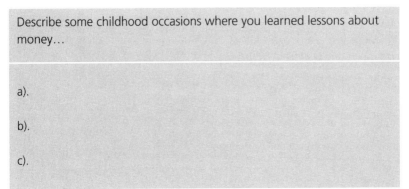

Describe some childhood occasions where you learned lessons about money…

a).

b).

c).

frivolous or something longer-lasting. One of the reasons we face such challenge as a nation of debtors is the easy access to credit cards and the apparent myopia over our spending. In spring 2002 the average debt was £8000 per household. This excludes home mortgages and vehicle finance.

Do take the time to think about these questions, using Fig. 2.1 and please don't push them away as psychobabble. To be successful in choosing, financing and buying just one property for investment or ten properties, you must have a strategy for dealing with the process. Be clear on this and you will get a great deal out of this book.

> To be successful in choosing, financing and buying just one property for investment or ten properties, you must have a strategy for dealing with the process.

A strategy for using money

When I speak to groups of landlords or to would-be investors in residential property it always surprises me how few people have a clear strategy for their role as landlords or would-be landlords. If you attempted to carry out your job with no game plan or procedural manuals and outside the law of the land, you would soon find yourself in trouble. Similarly, it would be impossible for you to run a profitable business without a business plan that had meaningful goals and was regularly updated and revised. Don't think that you can just pick up a property and receive a rent roll. It doesn't happen that way.

In the next few chapters I shall explain the way you can develop your own route into property investment, whether it is for you to buy your first investment property and work your way steadily to a second or if you are seeking to pick up a few tips and techniques for fast growth. The key is that you need to be very clear on the reasons you are investing in the first place. Work on this before you so much as go near an estate agency office or into an auction room. You will save yourself many thousands of pounds that you might otherwise have wasted.

Why this approach?

What this book is really about

In raising the subject of money and asking you about role models you may have had for money as you grew up, I am keen for you to begin to identify with the mental pictures you have about money, and in this context, about the investment of that money. Hopefully, you completed some of the basic exercises in the previous chapter that were designed to have you put down in writing your thoughts about the potential benefits that extra income would allow you to choose.

Most important is that you grasp the power of successful investing, whether it is in stocks and shares, known as 'equities', or in rental property described frequently as 'buy to let'. I personally always find this latter phrase to be inadequate because only professional letting agents refer to the process of letting. Most landlords and virtually all tenants refer to the process as renting, hence this book title.

The true power of investing is a function of recognising the way that money flows through life.

The job mentality

Consider the first group of the families I described in Chapter Two, those like my own, as an example. These people have a job mentality whereby they go to work day in, day out, and accept a value for their time that is determined by the boss or the company and is hopefully enough for them to keep a roof over their heads, pay the bills, and perhaps have enough each year to take an annual holiday. Harsher labels I have heard include the like of 'wage slaves' or people working a JOB, which is supposed to be short for 'Just over broke'.

Virtually all of us start our working careers in this way when we accept

Figure 3.1   Job mentality

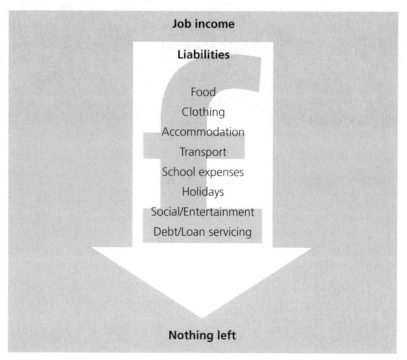

our first job. We begin with the understanding that this is what a job is, a means of paying the bills. Perhaps if we work harder than others do we shall have the opportunity to rise through the ranks. If this opportunity is not available, or not attractive to us, we hope that we can at least keep our job, bring home a regular wage, and take care of our needs and those of our family based upon the income we create. If we create less income we create less opportunity and we choose to cut our cloth according to the money that comes in from the job. If we look at the money that is earned in this scenario it flows through the family as in Fig. 3.1.

In this situation, life is a struggle. With each increase in the cost of living or rise in inflation there is another pinch felt in the household budget. Every time a new expenditure hits, we have to make a decision about where else in the budget can we make a reduction. The greatest challenge we face when we resign ourselves to being in this space is that we are starting each month in the same position or situation as we were in the previous month. Looking ahead one more month or one

> With each increase in the cost of living or rise in inflation there is another pinch felt in the household budget.

more year can be both depressing and demoralising because there is no way to see anything different happening, or to expect something more interesting or exciting to present itself.

A savings mentality

The next step up is where you can see the money coming in being used as widely as possible, taking care of daily living expenses and a small amount is passing into a savings programme, even while outstanding debts and loans are being paid down each month (see Fig. 3.2). What is crucial here is that hope is created by the saving of some money for the future. To be more specific, because you know you have money in a separate place other than just being absorbed by the daily grind, it is possible to be more optimistic and more focused upon the future.

Rather than being stuck in the nine-to-five job rut of home to work and work to home all the time, it is now possible to sense there is something else out there. The more hope there is the greater the energy you feel and the easier it becomes to think of managing the limited resources better.

Figure 3.2 Savings mentality

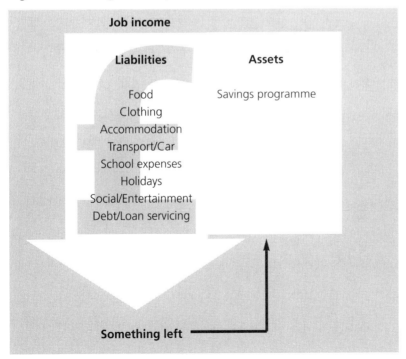

Figure 3.3   Investing mentality

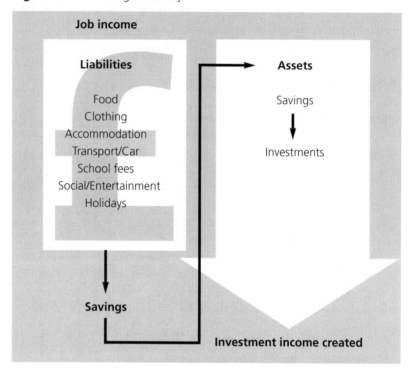

An investing mentality

Regular savings may accumulate to be enough to create an investment (see Fig. 3.3). This now produces a return in the form of a dividend, a rent roll or a regular income stream. You have also paid down the debt and loan commitments. With steady reinvestment, and bolstered by savings from job income, the returns on investments increase. These returns develop to become a separate income stream – asset income.

Business ownership mentality

Consider Fig. 3.4 and notice how different this cash flow is from the first one we looked at. Now the job income has disappeared because the job has gone by this stage! It is now business ownership dividends and continued investment income that is pumping the cash flow. By reaching this stage you have created the structure and the investment vehicle to provide a cash flow for as long as you require.

Figure 3.4 Ownership mentality

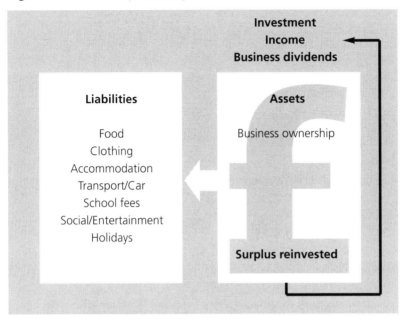

Different thinking produces different results

The idea that your thoughts create your reality has been around a long time. In the previous figures we have looked at how your thinking and the patterns of behaviour you adopt with regard to your money determine what your money does for you. We have seen how easily you can move your circumstances around to meet the goals you have set for yourself.

Do you want it to work in your favour, or to fizzle out before you have even paid the monthly bills? It takes discipline to become a successful saver, and then the same discipline repeats itself until you become a successful investor. The amounts of money get larger but the principles of investing that you use remain the same.

If a person spends money on something that yields no long-lasting return, the money is wasted. Examples of this might be buying more food than you will eat and throwing some away; renting videos instead of recording them from the TV and watching them when you have the time; buying a car that you cannot afford on credit rather than buying a slightly older and less fashionable car with money you can afford and without the extra cost of finance. If you spend money on a trashy novel or a cinema ticket the chances are you can enjoy the book and see the film, but be no better off afterwards, either practically or mentally.

None of these habits is doing you any good. The excessive purchase of food does not help either your health or your self-esteem and the purchase of a car on finance when you have other loans only serves to place you deeper into a debt trap, from which it will be more and more difficult to escape.

Using money like this creates nothing new and positive. Such use of money is 'soft' and it melts away until there is nothing left. A kind of easy come, easy go philosophy to spending.

> An investment mentality is about using money in a way which means it replaces itself all the time and is not squandered.

By contrast, an investment mentality is about using money in a way which means it replaces itself all the time and is not squandered. An example might be using money to invest in a place in an evening school. Here you learn a new subject, or you learn about an existing topic from a new and different angle. The learning improves your performance in the work place and you receive a pay rise as a direct result of your new learning. You re-invest this in more education and you become stronger mentally as well as financially.

Investment mentality thinking would stop you from buying a new car on borrowed funds until the debt on the previous one was paid off. It could also mean that you identify ways you can use your car to pay for itself, or that you follow methods of getting tax relief on your car expenses and costs when you might previously not have bothered.

The key to you being able to start developing strong income from property rental lies in how you use the money you have. It does not really matter how little you have as surplus each month. But it does matter that you start to use the power of compound interest to work for you and each amount of money you have to invest. Returns of 15 per cent and above are easy to achieve by looking around before you follow the herd.

This is at odds with some of the more conventional thinking on the subject of buying to rent and investing in property. As recently as February 2002, a columnist in the *Financial Times* wrote that unless you have a million pounds or more to invest there is little point getting involved with a rental property portfolio. This was in the same edition that another writer suggested that 7 per cent would be a very high return to achieve! How wrong can 'the experts' be?

It is a good thing that the people whose stories I highlighted in Chapter Two had not heard such advice. Most of them started with a combination of little or no money and a lot of common sense.

Your approach to duplication

The focus here is on the creation of a business that will give you the opportunity to duplicate your time and the scope to create income streams. Most businesses never manage the first step of duplicating themselves. Obvious exceptions are many of the world's most successful franchise brands. The franchisee buys into a system of teaching and training that has been developed previously by the franchisor. The quick access to this accumulated knowledge is what gives the franchise owner the opportunity to learn from mistakes that have already been made. This leaves them free to concentrate on the purpose of the business – making money and profits for the family.

If your goal is to buy one house or to buy three it is crucial you understand what the money does, how it works and how much the income from each property affects your earnings and gives you fresh options.

With one house providing an income, however small, you can begin the process of duplication for yourself. Now the goal is to duplicate the income you have from working. Look at Fig. 3.5 about Michael. I wrote about him in Chapter One. He has four terraced houses and is 23 years old.

Michael's work income each month is around £700 after tax. The gross income from rental of £250 adds a third to his income, or 16 per cent a month when recorded gross after the outgoings. This basic calculation may lack detail, but gives an idea of the revenue and costs involved. He

Figure 3.5 Michael

Work income	£11 000	
First house	Terraced house with two bedrooms	
Purchase price	£22 000	
Deposit	£2 200	(10% of purchase price)
Legal fees	£350	
Decoration	£300	(Painting and simple cleaning)
Monthly mortgage	£120	(6% mortgage)
Buildings insurance	£15	
Per month		
Total outgoings	£135	
Rental income	£250	
Gross monthly profit is about £115, or £1380 a year		

has four properties in the same town. He has bought them for between £22 000 and £30 000 and the total monthly rent received is £1100 gross. The money he is left with after mortgage payments and insurance is still £600 and matches 85 per cent of his take-home pay.

Aged 23 and getting on with his job, Michael is quietly buying terraced houses to a formula he knows he can afford. He already has an income from his job and his investments to match that of his supervisor at work. Just four more properties of a similar nature purchased over the next three years will put him in a position to be able to have more choices.

Perhaps he will choose to gain more education, while the rental stream pays for his college fees. Possibly he will start to buy three-bed houses that achieve higher rent and have a bit more diversity in his portfolio of houses. He may even stay in his job until he can start a business of his own doing something totally different to his current job. The point is that he is in control of his finances and has begun to duplicate his work income. In the event that he suffered a serious illness or was unable to work, he has become financially independent.

The price Michael paid to do this? Eight deposits of less than £4000 each and after the first three these deposits were paid for by cash flow from the first houses he purchased.

Now, look at Nicola's situation, summarised in Fig. 3.6. Her work income each month is about £1800 after tax. The gross income from

Figure 3.6 Nicola

Work income	£35 000	
First house	Town house in busy market town on the Thames	
Purchase price	£160 000	
Deposit	£40 000	(25% of purchase price)
Legal fees	£1 000	
Decoration	£2 000	(Painting and simple cleaning)
Building work	£21 000	To create three flats
Revaluation fee	£200	
Monthly mortgage	£850	(£141 000 @ 6% mortgage)
Building insurance	£50	
Per month		
Total outgoings	£900	
Rental income	£1 800	from the two rented flats
Gross monthly profit is about £900, or £10 800 a year		

rental brings in £1800 or the equivalent to her net work income. By risking the money she borrowed from family and a small inheritance to pay for the deposit, the legal fees and the decorating costs, she was able to buy the property. The cost of architectural plans, building work and internal renovation to make three small flats inside the property set her back a further £21 000. The increased value of the property allowed her to put this on the new mortgage she had taken out.

Now she has been able to rent out two of the flats to working couples at £900 per month. She has created an income of £1800 a month from this, allowing her to live comfortably on the salary she had before when she was renting a flat herself. She has effectively acquired an asset for the cost of her gambling the deposit money on the investment. She was lucky and it paid off for her. She owns a large property containing three separate living units. If she chose to, now that she has bought herself a place on the property ladder, she could move out of her flat, rent this for another £800 to £900 per month and have an income of £2600 per month. Within six months she could pay back the money borrowed from her family and would then be free to consider buying more investment property.

Over the next three years, her revenue from rental would be £93 000. It would have been bought with what now seems like a very small amount of borrowing and would provide her with the opportunity to consider buying a house that was her own and had no other tenants or sub-divisions within the building. This was her original goal. From being stuck in a rut Nicola has moved into financial stability through a bit of lateral thinking over the use of the property she bought.

This is a strong example of what is achievable with the use of a deposit and some imagination. I hope the illustration has shown how you can be more open-minded about what you expect from property investment.

Hopefully, these two simple scenarios have helped you to consider your own circumstances and provided some practical inspiration. Perhaps they have also laid to rest one of the worst myths about property investment – that you have to have a lot of money to get started. You don't need the money because you can borrow it sensibly. You do need the formula or the strategy to support your goals.

The money facts about life in Britain

According to the newspapers and the glossy magazines, we have 'never had it so good', live in 'the land of plenty' and as a nation have been called 'the rich man of Europe'. Where is the evidence for this?

How the wealth stacks up

Perhaps more than any other nation, Britain has a fascination with the ownership of land, and along with this the ownership of property. In England alone there are about 5000 landed estates with an average of two square miles each and worth £4 million per estate. The top 20 land-owning families have enough land to absorb the counties of Essex, Kent and Bedfordshire with space left over. This contrasts strongly with the Irish experience where the land-owning class has been virtually removed from the picture.

One of the challenges produced by this distribution of wealth is the vast rise in land prices. Kevin Cahill, author of *Who Owns Britain*, has commented that as much as a half to two-thirds of the cost of building a property is taken up by the cost of the land. The failure of any land redistribution processes over previous centuries has left a legacy of overvalued land where it comes onto the market. The astonishing disparity is easily seen in the gap between wealthy estates that are measured by the square mile and the more normal size of housing space where the majority of us survive within a land space of just 340 square yards.

The biggest leisure spenders in Europe

United Kingdom gross domestic product per head is higher than that of

Germany and France and all other members of the European Union. While some of this has come about as a result of the strength of the pound against a weaker euro, the main factor is the underlying strength of the economy, which in 2001 grew faster than any other leading industrial country.

We spend more on leisure and holidays than others in Europe. Our top priorities as a nation are now drinking, socialising, eating out and taking holidays. However, if we cannot afford to pay for such luxuries from our own money we are now the most likely to reach for a credit card.

We are working longer hours

The fast increase in incomes in the UK over the past decade has been paralleled by the working of longer hours and the decline of the traditional family structure, ensuring we have more spare cash left over for our social lives.

As people are now having children later in their lives – closer to 30 years old than 20 – many now have an extra ten years of freedom and they spend their income accordingly. Likewise, the growth in divorce looms large as more middle-aged people are now single again and want to go out socialising after work, rather than rushing home. Figure 4.1 shows how we spend our money.

How we spend our money

We are spending an average per household of £3410 a year on our leisure and pleasure. By comparison the French figure is £1873 and the Italian number is £1712 per household.

The worrying side-effect of all this leisure spending is the increase in the core debt on household credit cards. This refers to the amount of debt that is not paid off each month, but recycled through another month, with the payment of interest to the card companies. As this goes up, we may see more people unable to invest in their own property, or who choose to 'downsize' to a smaller property and draw out equity to repay debt. This creates more opportunity for the would-be landlord to provide good quality accommodation to the rental market.

> The worrying side-effect of all this leisure spending is the increase in the core debt on household credit cards.

Figure 4.1 How we spend our money

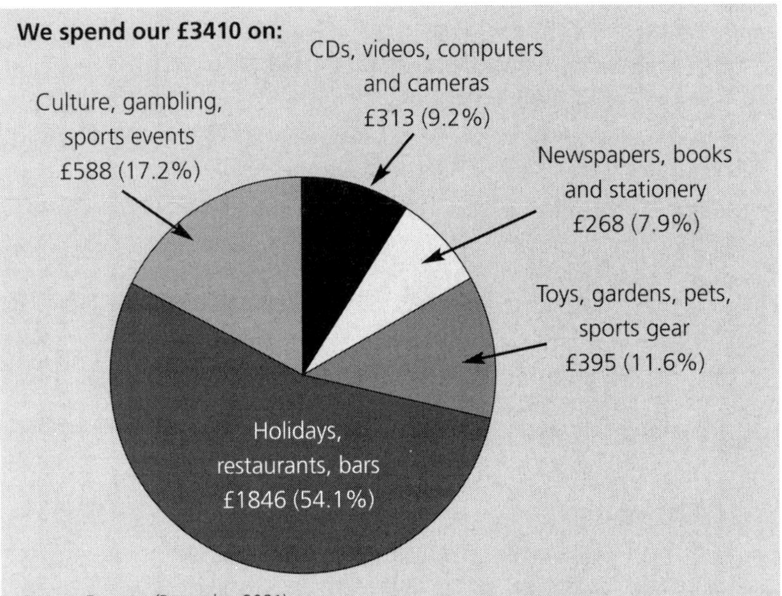

Source: Eurostat (December 2001)

But figures and statistics such as these should also be a warning sign to us that there is an enormous financial catastrophe waiting to happen should we be unable to work due to ill-health or lose our jobs. If we are unable to generate income from our work, most of us can survive for less than six months on what are otherwise considered good levels of saving.

The cost of children

If the figures about average spending on leisure and social activities are not enough to raise concern, then consider figures published in January 2002 by the *London Magazine* as a result of a survey on the cost of living in the capital. They are frightening by any standard.

Admittedly, they are focusing on an affluent group of people who are high-income earners and who have high family and social aspirations. That aside, the implications of these findings should set alarm bells ringing for families with even modest aspirations. Looking only at the costs involved in raising a child from birth until graduation from university aged 21 years, the survey considered the costs of the most basic of care provision as well as the expense of clothing, toys, hobbies and pocket money.

Figure 4.2   The cost of raising a child in London

First year		Cost (£)
Basic feeding equipment, food, clothing and toys		2 840
Changing equipment and nappies		800
Nursery equipment		1 300
Basic safety equipment (stair gates, fireguards)		200
	Sub total	5 140
Years 1–5		
Clothes, food, toys and other expenditure		12 000
Pocket money (average of £6 per week)		1 248
Nursery (for two years at £4000 per year)		8 000
	Sub total	21 248
Years 5–11		
Private day school for six years		43 000
Uniform and sports kit		1 248
Extra activities: hobbies, music, trips, etc		6 120
Clothes, food, toys, and other expenditure		18 000
Pocket money		1 872
	Sub total	75 192
Years 11–18		
Private day school for seven years		50 400
Uniform and sports kit		7 000
Extra activities: hobbies, music, trips, etc		7 140
Clothes, food, toys, and other expenditure		31 500
Pocket money		2 184
	Sub total	98 224
Years 18–21		
University fees and living expenses for three years		25 125
	Sub total	25 125
TOTAL		**£224 929**
With inclusion of either babysitting or nanny		£317 857

Source: London Magazine

Even if you strip away the costs of private schooling and education (included here as a total of £101 400), then the total before babysitting or nanny costs is still an enormous £123 500 per child. Assuming that you don't happen to be one of those people who have £120 000 sitting idly in the bank and paying you £6000 a year in interest, and which you need for no other reason, how can you create £6000 a year? And what if you did want a private education for your child? Now you will need to have £240 000 in the bank with no other claim to its interest to match the figures and the costs hinted at by the London survey.

If you think that childcare costs and babysitting is the price you want to pay – either to enable both parents to stay in their well-paid and secure jobs or to allow for permanent home-based childcare support while one partner stays at home – then there will be little money to spare after you receive the annual interest on your £240 000, which earns you 5 per cent.

Dual-income, middle-class households are finding it increasingly difficult to manage to enjoy the lifestyle they were expecting. Aspirations coming out of university were for the home, the cars, the foreign holidays and the trappings of a successful working role. Instead, more and more are learning the need to cut back on their spending if the children's experience of growing up is not to be tarnished.

One of the problems here is that the childhood's we may have thought we experienced in terms of seeing our parents together each night, of family time spent together at the weekends, has fallen victim to the trends that see us working ever longer hours to meet the basic targets we set ourselves. Did our parents ever face the choice of consumable goods that are available for us to throw our money at? Did they have the borrowing facilities in the form of easy loans and credit cards?

Either we learn to set simpler and more meaningful financial targets or else we must acknowledge the limits to what we can achieve while remaining healthy and sane.

And we are living longer

For people who began their working careers after the start of the 1950s and who regularly contributed to their company pension fund, the benefits they have received have been far more than expected. Blue chip investments saw many of them retire in the past 15 years able to enjoy their gardening years confident in the knowledge they could look forward to a steady pension each month, free to enjoy hobbies and pastimes after 40 years of a working career. They have done well and are naturally pleased with their circumstances.

But this cosy approach to retirement is not one that can be maintained. The biggest reason is the fall in average expected mortality rates. In other words, we are living longer and more money will be needed to support these longer lives. If a person retiring at 65 was expected to live for perhaps six or seven more years to reach their early seventies, and is now living into their late seventies or even their eighties, then the money from the pension companies is under far greater pressure than before. Our living longer places a huge demand on the pension funds that were not foreseen by the actuaries who manage and control them.

With pay outs being higher than expected, many companies have looked at ways to close down guaranteed or defined pensions to new staff and instead offer pensions linked with investment performance. This reduces the threat of the existing pension pot being drained before the already retired group have drawn their monies from the fund. The worry is that some pension funds have underestimated by as much as 30 per cent the amount of provisions required to be in a fund if it is to continue to pay out to the retired.

No wonder the government is keen for people and companies to be involved in stakeholder pension schemes, which collect and administer the funds from within new company programmes.

> If we are living longer, there are fewer people in the work-force contributing to the government's fund for pension provision.

The other issue of pension funding that is a function of us living longer is the problem of who is putting into the pot. If we are living longer, there are fewer people in the workforce contributing to the government's fund for pension provision. Currently there are four workers for every pensioner in the European Union. Twenty years ago there were six workers per pensioner. By 2050 there will be just two. This is a staggering decline in the number of workers able to contribute to government programmes and gives further evidence of why governments are promoting stakeholder pensions.

What it all means to you

Longer lives, more social and leisure spending, lower investment returns and reduced pension benefits mean just one thing – a poorer and more uncertain retirement. If the cost of living continues to increase, however slowly, and the ability of most people to save consistently from their earnings is very low, then the need for borrowing can only go up. As we borrow more money to live on we get ever deeper into debt and struggle to escape the crippling trap that comes with such borrowing.

At a time when dignity should be high after a working career, the threat of living in poverty and struggling through retirement has become very real. In his Budget speech of 1998, Gordon Brown, Chancellor of the Exchequer, was brave enough to talk publicly about the fact that half the population of Britain have less than £200 of savings. Just £200. Such shocking figures show the true extent and effect of poor financial education. Rather than be personally stuck with such sad consequences for your own later years, take steps now to learn about money management and the creation of strong financial assets for the benefit of you and your family.

There is an enormous gap between the figure of £200 in savings and the needs of a family for a working lifetime that is followed by a lengthy retirement. The ability of the government to finance that gap is just not there. The options for personal borrowing from a bank or other lender to bridge the gap will never exist. We are already working such long hours that we do not have the chance to squeeze more time into the day. Even if you do manage to find extra hours from your social life or your family time, the rate you get paid per job is deliberately held down by the employer so you are really no better off.

Building your asset base

The only way to create the financial income stream that will be required in future years is for you to take time and effort to understand how to create and build assets that throw off regular cash month after month. By building these assets, however slowly, you are stepping out of the trap of working for money and of exchanging your valuable time for a wage determined by someone else.

In the example at the start of this chapter, the cost of raising a child was calculated at about £5000 a year without including private education; double this figure if the education is to be bought rather than delivered by government in exchange for the taxes you pay.

A simple £50,000 3-bed semi-detached property available in many parts of Britain either representing good value or else after successful negotiation on a distressed property. A simple £50,000 3-bed semi-detached property, available in many parts of Britain as a good value buy or as a distressed property in need of some work, will give you a gross return of at least £600 a month or £7200 a year before mortgage costs.

Obviously there are other purchase and legal costs and you will have to declare the income so as to be taxed on it. Yet, you can clearly see that you have begun a process of creating cash flow from an asset. Over the same 21-year period that the London example quoted for the costs of raising a child, your house will throw off income of £150 000. This is a simplistic figure that does not include price increases but is a huge contributor to the education and upbringing of your child.

chapter five

The reason why

C hapter Four explained why people in general need to be developing independent income streams, but why do you want to do this? Are you looking to become wealthy?

If this is a goal for you, keep reading because ownership of surplus property has long been one of the characteristics of wealthy people. Knowing you have surplus property assets can make it easier for you to borrow money for other projects, as well as obviously giving you the additional income stream from rental.

Why this might appeal to you

There may be as many reasons to do this as you can ever imagine, but let's take a look at the whole sector and consider what this could do for you.

■ You get the benefit of a regular and valuable income stream as a return on your capital investment.

■ Your property is kept occupied, heated and looked after, reducing the need for you to worry about leaving it empty.

■ If you need to relocate to a job many miles away, or even overseas, you can focus on making the right career decision, free from the distraction of thinking 'What about the house?'

■ Using a management company takes away the need for you to be involved in collecting rents, sorting out repairs and decoration, or dealing personally with tenants.

■ An inherited property that you love need not be sold and can stay within your family for future generations.

■ A property with tenants in it is regularly inspected, and will be maintained better than if it were empty. In this way your original investment is protected soundly.

Protection

If you lost your job next week how safe would your home and your lifestyle be? If this were to happen and the job was gone, how long could you survive? Two months, a month, three weeks? Are you mortgaged to the hilt or do you have a large pot of savings just for 'rainy days' like these? If you do lose your job, how quickly could you expect to be back in another job and how close would the new job be financially to the one you lost? Be realistic in thinking about these questions. Large numbers of people have no unemployment or redundancy protection on their mortgages. For those who have this policy, the process can take a few months before it 'kicks-in' and once the payment protection starts it would usually last just a year.

Could you be one of the people who are borrowing three or four times earnings to have bought your house? If so, just consider the problems that could come about with a small rise in interest rates. If you are struggling to pay monthly bills, please don't rush into an investment property. Pay down your debt and negotiate more affordable repayments with lenders on your personal finance borrowings. But while this is happening, maintain a watchful eye for opportunities with property that might allow you to get started, steadily developing a cash flow to help you.

See money saved now towards a property to rent as an antidote to something dreadful like redundancy happening in your future.

What do you long for in your life?

No silly answers now! The more definition in your vision for what you want your circumstances to look and feel like, the easier it will be to find this place. We can't all be driven by the same sources of motivation so it will help to know more about your reasons for seeking the goals you have in mind.

If we are not all chasing higher salaries, better working conditions and more holiday time then what are we after? Some of us are driven by career achievement and success; others by important causes and projects we care about; while still more of us seek to pursue a lifestyle that we feel is right for us. How do you fit in to Fig. 5.1?

Figure 5.1 What drives you?

Career-driven person	You want to generate more money. Personal success and the recognition of that achievement is important to you. You have high ambition levels and you love to talk about work issues. You get a buzz from being busy and involved
Cause-driven person	You want to make a difference in the lives of others and to be making your own contribution. However small it may be, it is important that you are doing it. If it has social value then it can be worthwhile following it through. You talk keenly of your cause or causes and the reasons why I should be joining you on your path
Lifestyle-driven person	Just so long as it is fun and enjoyable you'll be there. 'Let's have an investment property provided it is not too much hassle!' You want to work at something you enjoy rather than become a slave to others who don't appreciate your talent. You need your freedom and tell us so!

Give yourself more options

As you develop a portfolio of properties, the scope for you to increase the measure of the benefit also expands, such that you may be able to replace a full-time career with several houses or flats rented out. Perhaps you could maintain your work, yet have additional income to enjoy better holidays while reinvesting a large proportion of the rental monies received. All very good and interesting reasons but take a look at this next one. It must surely be the best kept secret of the wealthy, yet it is so simple to observe and apply.

The power of compound interest

Most people have no understanding of the power of compound interest. You have – and you need to focus on the many practical and social benefits this can bring to you.

The easiest way to accumulate money is to ensure that you spend less than you earn and you invest the balance.

In the case of equity investments the approach might be called 'a buy and hold' strategy where the investor buys equities in 'blue chip', well-regarded corporations, receives dividends twice a year and reinvests these to purchase more shares. Over time it is natural to expect the revenue from this portfolio to begin to yield meaningful dividends.

With cash that is saved and invested in banks and financial institutions, they borrow the money from you, make a return on it through their own investment strategies and guarantee a small return on your money. Provided you maintain the money with them they will give you greater levels of interest. These levels of return are directly related to the amount of time you have agreed to lock-in your money with them. Your money compounds to become larger because of the interest you are paid.

A simple illustration of this is the ancient Chinese story of the warlord who was asked by his emperor to defend the kingdom from attack and who was asked to name his price for his services. The retelling says that the warlord asked for one small bag of rice on the first day, two bags on day two and four on day three, with the doubling of his payment in rice each day. Although seen as a valuable item, a bag of rice to begin with seemed an easy price to pay for his services and the emperor agreed. Of course, long before the end of the military campaign the payments to the warlord were so great that he had effectively taken control of the rice supplies for the whole territory.

The compounding effect of rental income

In the context of rental income the power of compound interest works like this. Assuming a net rental income of £400 per house per month after costs, here is an illustration of how one house becomes four properties in less than four years. Note that this is without you borrowing excessively, and without you taking any positive equity from your own property to invest in additional properties.

The other assumption is that the houses or flats being purchased are at £40 000 each requiring a deposit of 25 per cent or £10 000 per property, and that you are managing to save £300 a month in your property account. In respect of house prices increasing I have included increases in the amount of the deposit required over time.

Figure 5.2 shows how you created four properties and a positive cash flow at the end of four years of more than £4000 per quarter, or in excess of £19 000 a year. At the same time as doing this you have created four assets that are yours to keep and which the tenants in each property are paying off for you over time.

Also remember that in this example the income was created from your

Figure 5.2

Cash flow Outflow (£)	Q1	Q2	Q3	Q4	Q5	Q6	Q7	Q8
Deposit 1	10 000							
Deposit 2							10 000	
Inflow								
Rental	1 200	1 200	1 200	1 200	1 200	1 200	1 200	2 400
Savings	900	900	900	900	900	900	900	900
Your account	2 100	4 200	6 300	8 400	10 500	12 600	4 700	8 000

Outflow (£)	Q9	Q10	Q11	Q12	Q13	Q14	Q15	Q16
Deposit 3		12 000						
Deposit 4					15 000			
Inflow								
Rental	2 400	3 600	3 600	3 600	3 600	4 800	4 800	4 800
Savings	900	900	900	900	900	900	900	900
Your account	11 300	3 800	7 900	11 800	16 300	7 000	12 700	18 400

initial £10 000 deposit on a single property. Perhaps now you can see that many landlords will quietly laugh when they read in the press of the potential for returns as high as 7 per cent on investment property! And you didn't need to invest your £1 million to do so.

To some people the numbers discussed will seem falsely small, and if you are one of these people you are in a fortunate minority. Yet, if you do your research you will begin to realise how vast the market is for you to purchase a few properties and create an income stream for yourself. Figure 5.3 is for you to conduct your own sample cash flow forecast. For example, you may live in a town where a starter property can only be bought for £100 000. If this is the case, then run the figures on £100 000 and a £25 000 deposit. But also remember to factor in a monthly rental that is higher, perhaps £600 to £800 a month. Work through the process here, or in a simple spreadsheet on your computer to begin to see the benefits.

Supplement your job or career

This was precisely how we got started. I was working for a bank in a role I no longer enjoyed and where I felt that people were always taking advantage of me. I saw classified adverts in the evening papers and in

Figure 5.3 Your own example

Cash flow Outflow (£)	Q1	Q2	Q3	Q4	Q5	Q6	Q7	Q8
Deposit 1	?							
Inflow								
Rental								
Savings								
Your account								

Outflow (£)	Q9	Q10	Q11	Q12	Q13	Q14	Q15	Q16
Inflow								
Rental								
Savings								
Your account								

local shops for rooms to rent. Well, I had a spare room in my house and I was struggling to pay the mortgage with ease. Looking at the numbers it looked like an easy game to get paid to let someone else use that room.

I placed a classified advert in the local paper and spent the next few evenings showing people round the house and explaining what was available. When I met someone who I thought would suit the house, we went ahead and they moved in. Not exactly a scientific process, but it worked well enough for me to repeat the process several times.

With hindsight, that first time I rented a spare room was the beginning of the process of becoming a landlord and many of the things I know today started to make sense then. Having a little bit of extra income gave me the confidence to feel better about my circumstances. I could see that it was possible to have more control over my situation than I had felt before. This came as a big boost to my self-esteem.

If you could make the equivalent each month to replace a week of your income this would very likely give you great opportunities. It could pay for some of your social life. Perhaps it would provide you with the chance to take up a sport or an educational course. Explore all the avenues you can think of.

Grab a sheet of paper and write down the ways that you could imagine yourself enjoying extra income from property rental. The power of this exercise is that you almost immediately start to feel what it will be like to have this money coming in to your life and to your bank account. Once you have begun to see this extra income in your mind's eye, you are

Figure 5.4

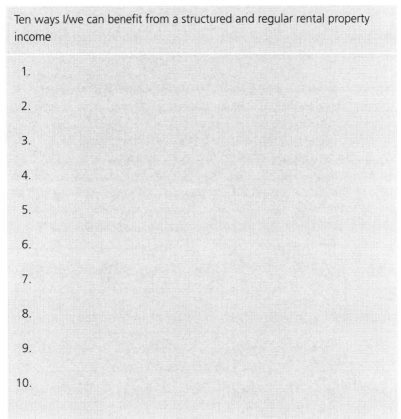

Ten ways I/we can benefit from a structured and regular rental property income

1.

2.

3.

4.

5.

6.

7.

8.

9.

10.

well on the way to having it happen. Remember the importance of seeing and being able to describe the picture you see.

> Once you have begun to see this extra income in your mind's eye, you are well on the way to having it happen.

How about selling properties?

If you just buy a new investment property every two years, then at the end of ten years you will end up with five or possibly more houses in your portfolio. Do you think the chances are good that at least two of the houses could have received a significant growth in their valuation? If you could sell one house for a large gain perhaps every three years, would the income from such a sale be really useful? Based on the money realised from such a sale it might be realistic to be able to live comfortably on the regular sale of such assets.

What about re-investing?

Imagine you had bought a property for £80 000 and after a number of years this increased to £120 000. Do you think you could sell the property and realise the £40 000 in cash? You probably could.

Another smart thing to do might be to re-mortgage the first property for, say, £60 000 of the £120 000. Now you have £60 000 to use as a good deposit on perhaps three more small properties, but which you know you can rent out easily. The cash flow from the three new houses, when added to the ones you already hold, could mean you have a strong monthly income after expenses that gives you great freedom of choice about where you live and why. The net rental gain from having the three new properties is far greater than the slight inconvenience of paying more in mortgage to cover the extra £60 000 borrowed by re-mortgaging.

Think about your motivations for doing this. Write them down in Fig. 5.5. Calculate their costs in Fig. 5.6.

It is not only when you are buying objects that you mentally view the price tag. Remember too that if you have made some notes about a

Figure 5.5

What are the three biggest reasons you can write down as important motivators for you to do this? Put them down on paper right now
1.
2.
3.

Figure 5.6

What about the cost or the price of acquiring these things you have just written down?
1.
2.
3.

Figure 5.7

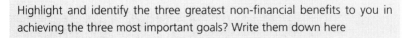

Highlight and identify the three greatest non-financial benefits to you in achieving the three most important goals? Write them down here

1.

2.

3.

lifestyle or way of living that would work better for you, you can identify a measurable non-financial value to this also (*see* Fig. 5.7).

Summary

Here are some other reasons you might want to take control of successful investing in buy to rent property.

- To have more control over my circumstances.
- To create financial freedom for myself and for my family.
- To build a business of my own.
- To create a legacy we can pass on.
- To be in a position where I can provide financial aid for others.
- To develop peace of mind by leaving the 'rat race' behind.
- To build insurance against an uncertain world.
- To develop the revenue to acquire some beautiful things.
- To buy back my time and my use of this time.
- To be free to work at what I love to do.
- To relax in the knowledge that our financial needs are met.

LANDLORDS TALKING – DENVILLE

Denville and his wife Diane own a new, three-bed house they bought from the developer a year ago.

'As a serving member of the armed forces we move every couple of years. We rent our own house out so my family can travel with me on my postings. Most of these have been abroad. This also keeps our house occupied and pays the mortgage.'

'We bought our investment property to get on to the housing ladder and for somewhere to live when I retire from the army. Many service personnel buy their own house as an investment and then rent it out as service accommodation. We use a professional management company which looks after the investments of a number of service families.'

'If I had my time again I would have brought a property when I first joined the army and rented it out. The rent would have paid the mortgage by now and we would be sitting on some useful money.'

Overturning the myths

I t is the false beliefs that some people have about investing in bricks and mortar that continue to stop others from getting involved in building up a portfolio of property. People will tell you that the moment you become a landlord you will lose all privacy, begin to receive phone calls from complaining tenants late at night and return to the property to see your possessions destroyed and carpets ruined. Naturally, such unfavourable views will stop many would-be investors dead in their tracks and ensure that they never enter the marketplace.

Yet from those who are financially successful landlords and property investors you will hear that the opportunities outweigh the disadvantages and that if you deal with people in large numbers as tenants then you are bound to win some and lose some.

Don't let fear hold you back. I say this based on experience, whereas more often than not the more negative comments are based on fear of the unknown, of perceived risk, or of change and come from a base of ignorance.

Crabs in the fishing pot

I remember the stories of the crab fishermen from childhood holidays in the south-west of England. Crabs climb into the string pots and baskets that are lowered to the sea bed. Once they are in the basket there is easily enough space and opportunity for a few of the crabs to clamber onto those covering the bottom of the basket, and to climb out, but the crabs attempting escape are frequently pulled back down into the basket by the others.

It seems often the same with grown adults – they want you to succeed as long as it's not beyond their own achievements! Whether it is a crab pot or a dinner table, people hold strong, and often unpredictable views on a subject and you shouldn't always expect them to agree with you. What matters is that you decide upon a strategy of investment that works for you; a strategy that is in line with your investment ideas and longer-term personal and financial goals, and that will allow you to enjoy peace of mind. There is little value to be had in investing outside your comfort zone, overstretching yourself financially, or creating disharmony at home through rigidly sticking to your own ideas at the expense of the tolerance of your partner's views.

Here are a few of the most frequently heard myths and assumptions that seem to put people off entering the marketplace. I hear these constantly and hope to remind you through explaining them that most myths are founded on lack of knowledge and poor awareness of the facts.

Myth 1 – There is no money in renting property

Yes! Some people actually believe this one! They usually know of a friend of a friend who had a bad experience and they cling to the view that they would go through the same troubles if they were to rent. While the stories like these stop some people coming into the property market as landlords, at the same time those who do step in feel protected that not everyone does this! There are a great many landlords creating returns of 15 per cent on their properties while others assume that they could not make money from the same circumstances. It all goes to show that one person's opportunity is another person's excuse.

Myth 2 – I can't trust anyone to get the rent in for me

And why should you be relying on just anyone? There is no point in being casual in your approach to collecting the rent. What matters is that you make a decision over whether you consider it worth collecting yourself, with all the effort this will involve, or whether you instead decide to pass the job on to a letting or a managing agent to take care of this for you.

> Your focus as a landlord seeking to run a profitable business is to see you do all that is right to ensure the tenant stays as long as possible.

Myth 3 – There is no such thing as an honest landlord

Really? There may be some individuals who give the business of being a landlord a bad name, but they are few and far between. There is no point in comparing yourself to someone who doesn't care about their tenants and has no interest in the standard of properties rented out. Your focus as a landlord seeking to run a profitable business is to see you do all that is right to ensure the tenant stays as long as possible and enjoys a safe and well-maintained property they can call home. If you have no interest in maintaining these standards, don't even bother to start enquiring about what it takes to invest in residential property. You will be wasting your time.

Myth 4 – I have to use cash

You don't have to use cash. Lenders are queuing up to lend you their own funds in order to help you realise your dream of having a few properties. However, it does make sense to ensure you have a good deposit to put down and reduce the amount you need to borrow. Just get the balance right so that you can see the return on both your deposit and the monthly mortgage finance commitments paying you a safe return.

Myth 5 – No one will lend me the money

This is patently untrue. At the time of writing, more than 40 commercial mortgage lenders are happy to see you buy investment property with their funds and even more will provide commercial loans secured on property investment. While their criteria for lending and the amount of risk they are willing to take varies, there is strong recognition that a client with three or four houses successfully rented out is a good client to have.

Based on this belief that the person with the assets is worth looking after, you should have little trouble getting a lender to help you become a borrower! We'll show you how straightforward this process can be.

Myth 6 – The law on investing is complex

This is generally true and there is a reason for this. If it were too simple or the information you need to know were so readily available, everyone would be doing it and one of the great secrets of the affluent asset owners would be public knowledge. It takes time and effort and a lot of digging for information you may not have known before. But you can acquire the knowledge or pay professionals such as solicitors and accountants to hold your hand through the process of learning. Once you have learned the rules of the game you can keep reapplying them and continue to create additional cash flow and income for yourself.

Myth 7 – If I live in rented accommodation I cannot get an investment mortgage

Not true. You simply need to think smarter and you can even have this situation work to your advantage when it comes to your application for a mortgage. Besides, you have to step onto the property ladder at some point and provided you can satisfy the borrowing criteria for your funding then it is irrelevant that you live in a rented space.

Myth 8 – I have to give the lender control of my house to buy another house

A painful myth, but still untrue. You don't have to go to your existing lender for your first investment property, and many schools of thought would suggest you shouldn't do so anyway. You simply need to show you can cover the bills on the new property before they agree to provide you with the majority of the funding, putting an asset on to your balance sheet with their money.

Myth 9 – It is against a law for me to have a job and own several investment properties

Because we are taught so little about money during school, many people subconsciously think this may well be true. My manager when I worked for a bank used to think that it wasn't quite fair or proper that I should have even considered it appropriate to have a career and earn additional income outside of the work place. He somehow thought the company was doing me a favour by providing me with my job and that I was being disloyal by not having the bank as my sole source of income.

Myth 10 – My relatives would be suspicious

So why tell them? Seriously, unless you are borrowing money from your family what has your investment plan to do with them? If you are borrowing with them or from them, then you may as well look at ways you can work together. It is human nature that people will either applaud or criticise your efforts and success.

When it comes to family, my view is that they are best kept out of it, on the grounds of the popular saying that goes 'Too many cooks spoil the broth'. If

> When it comes to family, my view is that they are best kept out of it, on the grounds of the popular saying that goes 'Too many cooks spoil the broth'.

you on your own want to talk to a parent or close relative about it then please do. But if you and your partner both feel certain you should be taking steps now to protect your financial future then the first people to speak to about the investment should be bankers, accountants and tax advisers.

Myth 11 – Never buy at an auction

Here is an activity that at least allows the serious investors to enjoy the benefits they receive at auction. Because of the doubts about what goes on at auction, or the fear that scratching your eyebrow too much will see you buying a detached cottage by mistake, many people have not explored the benefits to be had from hunting through the auction catalogues.

Auctions can yield tremendous bargains and give you good savings on open market valuations. As with other aspects of property investment, you should do your homework on any house you are interested in before you bid. When the hammer falls, you want to feel confident that you have a winner on your hands!

Myth 12 – Owning investment property will make my tax position worse

On the contrary, there are benefits to be had from the proper taxation of a business income that will stand you in good stead compared to someone who is perhaps attempting to be beyond the law, or who at least is failing to claim for the various allowances possible.

Myth 13 – I think I've missed the boat

Despite press rumours every few years to suggest that there is no point in getting into the market anymore, there is always a market. Someone is always looking for a space to live in a new town before they know where they want to buy. While someone is getting divorced they may want to consider their options carefully before knowing what size of house they want or to know what they can truly afford to buy. One person moving away from home means another looking for a job in the same town or city. Wherever people live there will always be demand for decent and affordable rental property.

The saddest thing about uninformed speculation on this topic is simply that people follow each other to feel safe. Sometimes too many people buy in a certain area or a trend is created because the loudest voice suggests that the solution is such and such an idea. Of course the people who jump last into a trend always feel let down. In London and the south-east recently there has been a rush to buy 'off-Plan' (a deposit to the builder speculating on the value of a property once it is completed and an option to sell as soon as the building is finished, or to find tenants quickly). This allows them to lock in to a good price long before their property is constructed.

Similarly, there was a rush to buy expensive and trendy apartments overlooking expensive and trendy areas in London. There is always a limit to the rent you can achieve and this is determined by people's wages that are sensibly limited by their companies.

Rather than worry that you have missed 'the boat', instead spend time looking at areas outside London or look at the areas where there is more demand for renting. These will primarily be suburbs and upcoming areas rather than areas already established. Look first for places where tenants want to rent and then later for places where you can get rent *and* capital appreciation.

As you can hopefully see, the opportunity that exists in overcoming these myths and the foolish thinking around the statements is easily remedied with a bit of common sense, a measure of intention and a willingness to ask questions.

LANDLORDS TALKING – MARIA

Maria has just sold one of the two rental properties she has bought over the past couple of years. She has kept hold of one flat in a small ex-council block of flats that is six storeys high. She has a buy-to-let mortgage through her bank, which was helpful about the process of lending for investment.

'I bought the flat from a friend who was already renting it out. I got it complete with furniture and tenants, although the tenants have changed twice since. My friend had originally purchased it to live in before renting. He sold it to me as he wanted the funds to invest in commercial property.'

Of the process, Maria says: 'I cannot recall where I first got the idea. I always thought buying property to rent was a good way to go. While I bought this privately from my friend I think the next one will be bought at auction.'

'The property I rented out previously was managed by an agent. They took 15 per cent plus VAT and did nothing that I could not have done. Now I advertise in *Loot* (a listings newspaper) and show the property myself. I have quite a bit of contact with the tenants when they first move in, but then hardly any, unless there's a problem.'

In describing her property investment goals Maria is clear that she would like 'one per year for the foreseeable future, with a blend of positive cash flow and equity growth'.

Maria saw the link between regular cash flow and the opportunity to 'write, speak, study (health related matters) and travel,' on the way to achieving financial freedom.

Wishing she had learned at an earlier age to save more, Maria expresses amazement 'at the number of people I have spoken to who could be doing this but won't because: they don't see themselves as "landlords"; they don't want the "hassle" (I've never had any); they can't be bothered; they'd rather spend the money on instant gratification (too short a time perspective)'.

chapter seven

How do you want to pay?

There are two ways to finance investment property and they affect your options and probably affect your attitude to risk at the same time. While the first can put you in total financial control of the purchase process, the second can provide confidence and reassurance to the more cautious investor. The first route is to take the cash you are prepared to invest and buy a property outright. The second is to borrow money from a lender with a loan that is specifically intended for you to buy an investment property.

Buying with cash

Cash investment is a great idea provided it does not put your own finances under any strain. For example, if you can take cash from your bank account and pay outright for a property without damaging your lifestyle then it may be worth considering.

Perhaps you have £100 000 in savings in the building society trying to earn decent interest. You see a property for sale at £60 000 that is in an area where you think there is good demand for rental property. Even after the purchase, you calculate you will have costs of perhaps £5000. This reduces your savings account to £35 000, on which you will continue to receive interest.

Do you think you can receive more on your £60 000 house in rental income than you would from the building society? Then consider going down this route.

But before you proceed, make sure the use of the cash is worthwhile. If you can get 5 per cent in the bank or the building society but 12 per cent to 15 per cent by renting out the house, then obviously you are better off putting the cash into the bricks and mortar. Yet how do you know you

> Ask around at estate agents' offices and letting agents to get a clear picture of what property is worth.

can get such a good return? Ask around at estate agents' offices and letting agents to get a clear picture of what property is worth in that condition and in that particular street. Don't buy too quickly just because you have money burning a hole in your pocket!

Developing your thoughts

Payback time. No, not a line from a bad film, but the way that professional investors will assess the benefits and the return of a particular property. You can see this rule being applied by investors when they are at auctions or when going through property details with an estate agent. They want to know how long they have to wait before the house has paid for itself.

An investor will look at a house, perhaps a three-bed property in a large town, and consider the potential rent. Will it bring in £600 a month? That is £7200 a year. If the property is valued at £60 000 then the gross rent is enough to pay the value of the house in just over eight years. If the same-sized property were to be for sale at £50 000 and the rent stayed the same, the payback period is down to less than seven years. If the original £60 000 house can be rented out at £800 a month or £9600 a year then the payback becomes slightly over six years. Using a process like this gives you a tool with which to judge your potential return on a property investment.

This is important given that most professional investors in residential property invest first for the cash flow that it provides and second for any potential capital growth. Most rental property will never experience huge price increases but will give steady returns.

London is a law unto itself in terms of the growth in property values relative to original purchase prices. Many friends have struggled in London to buy their first property and then experienced the rewards of big property price hikes that give great capital growth. If this is important for you, consider investing in more highly priced communities where the scope for growth in property value over a few years – say five or six – is part of your intention when buying the property.

However, if you, or your partner, are slightly nervous about taking that lump of hard earned cash to invest in a property (one of you may always feel safer to know you have cash behind you), then take the time to think a bit differently about the use of the money.

Borrowing the money

Have you got enough spare money for the deposit, legal fees and the trips you make to visit the property? The test here is, could you put that money to one side and mentally forget about it?

If a company employs you, are your managers willing to let you have a few days off or some extra hours so that you are able to keep on top of your solicitor about the stages of the purchase? Can you take time out in evenings and weekends to search different neighbourhoods, to paint and decorate, to collect rent? If you have to fund this time yourself, can you manage to do so?

Let's say this is a house which is purchased by you for £100 000. The figure is not the important aspect of this calculation. What matters is that you are going to have to find a large enough chest of money to pay legal fees to your solicitor, cover the costs of surveys and valuation reports, run around to accommodation and letting agents, pay decorators and builders, before knowing everything is done. As a rule of thumb, this means you needing to have the equivalent of three months in mortgage payments set aside.

Draw up a list of your own monthly spending and identify what can be used to cover the second mortgage each month. Here you are going to focus on every single penny not used wisely. Here is a place for you to look at your spending patterns and look at where you have surplus – or where you can see how you overspend – and trim back accordingly. Use the simple guideline shown here, but calculate the true numbers in each category in great detail. Collect spending information from your bank statements, store cards and credit cards. For the next two months write down every penny and pound you spend. You will probably surprise yourself!

> As a rule of thumb, this means you needing to have the equivalent of three months in mortgage payments set aside.

Don't be tempted here to think that you know what you spend just because you know what is left after your earnings. Look more deeply and record what you spend each day, noting the figure down each evening and starting again the next day. After a month of this you will hopefully have surprised yourself about where some of the money has been going, and how, with a little self-discipline, you can find more than you thought to go towards the deposit on your first investment property.

By creating a budget (see Fig. 7.1) you can learn to set aside the savings for a deposit on your first property for rental.

Figure 7.1 A basic budget

	Monthly total
1. Groceries and lunches	——————
2. Your own mortgage/rent	——————
3. Household utility bills	——————
4. Car running and service costs	——————
5. Leisure and social	——————
6. Clothing	——————
7. Family classes and training	——————
8. House maintenance bills	——————
9. Subscriptions/publications	——————
10. Laundry and dry cleaning	——————
11. Insurance	——————
12. Birthdays and Christmas	——————
13. Holidays	——————
14. Charitable donations	——————
15. Miscellaneous/Other	——————
Total	——————
× 12 = Annual total	——————

LANDLORDS TALKING – WILLIAM

'When we sold our embroidery business we kept the 150-year-old maltings building for ourselves. The 3500 sq. ft. property has commercial tenants. Last year we bought a four-bed house that we rent to students at the local university,' said William, who now works as an executive coach.

'We have mortgages on both properties. The maltings was bought with a second mortgage on our home and we have a buy-to-let mortgage for the terraced house.'

'We deliberately went into the student rental market to build up a pension fund as we don't have one and need to have something for our later years. We also wanted to leave some properties for our daughter so that future generations will have some capital to support their entrepreneurial desires if they have any. We have not based our strategy on anybody's and are just picking it up as we go along.'

Each property is professionally managed. 'We don't have the contacts, the time to interview tenants, or deal with all the legislation, the various registering authorities, the money aspect and we are not hard enough when one has difficult tenants. It is also very nice to have someone in the market to chat over a particular property that we are looking at.'

William encourages would-be landlords to think hard about entering the market. 'You have to think about the type of client, the level of breakages, where the rental money is coming from, for example, individual, corporate, council, or grant, and all the different levels of security and length of tenancy. It might sound negative, but before you start, consider that the type of tenant brings certain challenges – such as noise, drug usage, prostitution, parties, carrying on a business and illegal behaviour – all of which require a response from you.'

Funding a hobby while supporting the growth of his career is crucial to William and his wife Mary. 'We know the potential for developing passive income from our property and would love to develop a portfolio that generates sufficient income for me to develop my coaching practice and provide the funds to follow Formula One racing around Europe.'

'If we have a regret, it would be that we have not bought another property each year.'

Affording it

O ver the next ten years your salary is fairly predictable, assuming that you keep your job! Your home expenditure is also completely understood and within your control. Given these two things, and that you also know how the cost of living increases each year, it makes sense to put money into bricks and mortar. There is every likelihood over a ten-year period that the property will increase significantly in value. If you rent over the same period you will have no asset at the end of the period and the monthly rent is likely to have at least doubled every five years.

Can you really do this?

If you take a long view you will win. If you were buying a property for your child while they were at college or university for four years, does it make sense for other students and their parents to pay for your mortgage? At the end of the four years the property may have increased in value, and you will have a cash flow giving a profit after you have been paying down the mortgage. The real opportunity is for you to consider how much it might cost you if you used the same money, which you could put into a second property for other things. On the basis that you have worked out your budget and the amounts of money which you put into each of your expenditure categories each month, you should have a clear picture of where you have available money.

Getting started

One lender, recognising the huge gap between property prices in the south of England and people's inability to afford a first foothold on the property ladder, has introduced a mortgage where you can borrow a multiple of up to eight times your salary! There is, of course, a catch to this. The borrowing must be guaranteed or underwritten by a parent or close relative. The lender can then take comfort from the knowledge there is further security in the background. If you might qualify for such support then by all means discuss these possibilities with your family.

For the majority however, this is not an option and you need to explore other realistic possibilities.

The multiple mortgage

You can use a multiple mortgage to build up equity and buy your first property, or with one or two others you can invest in a rental property that none of you will live in. Lenders are attracted by this type of lending because they can see that when three people buy a property, each person only needs to find a third of the costs and so each person is putting less pressure than usual on their disposable income. Each investor also ends up with their one third share of an appreciation in value.

A case in point

Jason is a 26-year-old marketing manager working in Covent Garden in the heart of London. On his good salary of £24 000 most mortgage lenders will allow him to borrow between two and a half or three times his salary. Unable to buy himself a large flat for the £60 000 to £72 000 he could borrow, he rents a small one-bedroom flat in a relatively trendy area, but at a cost of £600 each month plus utility bills. Like most of his colleagues and friends at work, who are in the same situation, he believes he is in a trap. He can't afford to buy the starter property in an area close to where he works. If he moves out of town he could just afford a small property, but would then find he could not afford the cost of commuting. Catch 22 from which there seems little escape.

> Several commercial lenders will now accept applications from three or four borrowers on the same property.

What should he do? Remembering that the goal is to become a landlord by starting with his own property, Jason would do well to get a co-ownership mortgage with friends in the same situation. Several commercial lenders will now accept applications from three or four borrowers on the same property.

Co-ownership mortgages

Lenders want to feel secure that the loan will be repaid and will usually look to the two highest earners in the group when calculating how much can be borrowed. If the top two salaries are enough on their own, then the group can buy the property.

Lenders will look at the ability of the group to repay. The effect of this affordability approach is that it will allow your team to borrow more than the stricter method of looking only at income multiples. On this basis, a group of four people, each earning between £25 000 and £30 000, could look to borrow enough to buy a property worth £150 000 to £200 000.

Declaration of trust

Four people can be named on the deeds of the property but the declaration of trust is the vehicle to record the interests of these four and any others. While it might sound good that five or six friends can now buy a big house together, consider the practical difficulties inherent with so large a number. How long will you stay in the house? What happens when someone moves out, gets married or simply dies? These can be awkward matters to deal with, but each of them could wreck the situation unless thought through with care beforehand.

How you can help yourself

Have the largest deposit you can afford, say 10 per cent to 20 per cent between you. This will give some confidence to your lender because it shows your commitment.

What happens when one of the owners leaves?

When this happens their share can be sold to the person joining the others and you can take your share of the profits where the value has increased. Alternatively, the others who you first bought with can buy your share themselves at the current value. The person leaving should probably be the one to pay for the valuation of the property.

Final thoughts on co-ownership

Bear these points in mind before going ahead.

■ You need to get on well with each other, so it will help that you have been friends for some time beforehand.

■ Each person named on the mortgage deed will be jointly and individually liable to pay the whole mortgage. If one person fails to make the payments, the others have to pick up that share.

- Make sure that in the event of illness and not being able to work, you can still cover your share of the mortgage. If you don't already have it through your employer, consider getting critical illness cover or permanent health insurance, preferably both.

- If you get into arrears on such a mortgage, all of you will have your credit history marked with this poor payment record, even if you were the one who maintained your payments when the others didn't.

- Go to a solicitor and have a deed of trust drawn up between you. This will detail the original amount of investment put in by each person.

Where does the money go?

At the moment you may be spending a £100 or more a month on leisure or entertainment. On top of this there might be £100 on membership of a health or swimming club for example. Finally, there might be a similar amount each month being spent on impulse purchases such as clothes, chocolate, or sandwiches at work.

Use the budget planning tables (Fig. 8.1) to identify where you might be able to make savings, reduce some expenditure and divert the balance to a holding account to buy an investment property.

Although it takes time to gather together all the information you need for this exercise in such detail, the power of it is twofold:

- You have to face the financial realities of what you are spending.

- You then have a choice about how you maintain or reduce the amount of spending in a certain area.

Making your money work hard

With the example of you working through this exercise and finding a sum of say £300 per month or £3600 over the course of a year, you could purchase a property on which you could begin to achieve a monthly rental income of well in excess of £300 per month for as long as you want to into the future. Grasping the significance of this is not something that everyone will manage as they read this book.

Here is an example of the power of compound interest working for you. Your money will grow even when you are not there and when you have neither the time nor the energy to do anything with your funds. Take the example of the £300 a month we just mentioned. Put this figure each month into a savings account and let this grow at 6 per cent.

Figure 8.1   Budget planning in detail

Home outgoings	Weekly	Monthly	Quarterly
Rent or mortgage			
Building insurance			
Contents insurance			
Council tax			
Gas			
Electricity			
Water			
Telephone			
TV licence			
Repairs and renewals			
Other			
Total home outgoings			

Food, clothes, school	Weekly	Monthly	Quarterly
Food and groceries			
School fees			
School lunches			
Work lunches			
School uniforms			
Children's shoes			
Own shoes and clothes			
Partners shoes and clothes			
Casual clothes for children			
Other			
Total food, clothes and school			

Travel	Weekly	Monthly	Quarterly
Adult fares			
Child fares			
Visiting relatives and friends			
Car tax			
Car insurance			
Car servicing			
Petrol			
Other			
Total travel			

Financial	Weekly	Monthly	Quarterly
Bank charges			
Store card payments			
Credit card payments 1			
Credit card payments 2			
Loan repayments			
Pension contributions			
Life insurance			
Other			
Total financial			

Figure 8.1 (continued)

Other outgoings	Weekly	Monthly	Quarterly
Birthday presents			
Christmas presents			
Holidays			
Savings account			
Alcohol			
Cigarettes			
Meals and drinks out			
Subscriptions/memberships			
Prescriptions			
Child or spouse maintenance			
University and college fees			
Newspapers and magazines			
Miscellaneous			
Total other			

Summary of outgoings	Weekly	Monthly	Quarterly
Home			
Food, clothes and school			
Travel			
Financial			
Other			
Total outgoings			

Income	Weekly	Monthly	Quarterly
Wage or salary			
Commission			
Pension			
State benefits			
Maintenance receipts			
Other contributions			
Student loan income			
Rental income or lodger			
Other income			
Total income			

Final balance of income and outgoings	Weekly	Monthly	Quarterly
Total income			
Minus total outgoings			
Final balance figure			

Rental property for the older citizen

It is not just the young who have found it difficult to get on the property investment ladder. Senior citizens who may have finished their working career can also struggle to consider themselves able to invest in buy-to-rent property. A frequent assumption is that pensioners have no job or salary income and are therefore disqualified from borrowing for this purpose. However, with many lenders this is not the case at all.

> A frequent assumption is that pensioners have no job or salary income and are therefore disqualified from borrowing.

Many pensioners have provided for themselves in their retirement through a good pension scheme that provides them with an investment-based income. Lenders will consider this when looking at the borrowing for an investment property. A large number of lenders will support an application for investment borrowing based on the anticipated rental return. To save yourself time in the search for a mortgage lender who will lend against investment income you may be better off starting your search with a mortgage broker.

The usual principle applies of the rent being at least 130 per cent of the monthly repayment on the loan. Provided your rent matches this simple calculation you may find yourself able to borrow for an investment property of your own as a useful supplement to pension income and a potential nest-egg with capital growth for the future. Ask around.

Making money to help you make money

Often, people are convinced they are unable to manage an extra few pounds of savings or feel it is impossible to raise more cash for the deposit on their first investment property, however small. Be creative in looking at ways you can create more money.

Turn rubbish into another house

A couple looking to buy their third investment property went through their entire home over a weekend and were able to find two car loads of 'stuff' to get rid of including: books, videos, CDs, furniture, bicycles, unused wedding gifts, a TV, a cooker, crockery, a case of wine and various tool kits.

This everyday clutter raised several hundred pounds towards almost half of the £2000 deposit on a tidy terraced house that sold for £20 000 and produces a rent roll of £260 a month. What have you got hidden in your house that someone would willingly pay a few pounds for?

Could you work a few more hours in the month and develop overtime payments that added up to a couple of thousand pounds over the year?

Do you have skills or expertise that you are not using and which you could promote for a short period like a year in order to generate extra revenue towards that investment deposit? This could be teaching a specialist subject, providing a local or community service, or working at a local school for additional income. I know of several landlords who invest in a new property every year with the revenue from speaking fees they receive for delivering structured talks about interesting hobbies or travel experiences to groups during the winter.

Rent a room in your home

You are allowed under current legislation to have a tenant live in a room of your home and you can charge them for the privilege. What makes this so special is that the first £4250 of income each year will be treated as tax-free. Even where you think you are short of cash for investment, this amount of tax-free cash is an inspiration in getting a deposit ready.

Don't be precious about your first property

Where many people make a mistake with buying their first property is in trying to do too much on too small a budget. The usual warning signs are that they try to buy a property close to where they live, or similar in style. The same amount of space that in London suburbs would rent for £1000 a month and more might bring in just £400 elsewhere. Buying your first investment property in a cheaper community can allow you to buy a property with less cash. The rent is less but the yield on the investment is high because of the low purchase price.

When you buy to rent, do so with the focus on getting started successfully with a profitable investment, however small it may be, as opposed to an expensive investment.

LANDLORDS TALKING – ROGER

Roger and his wife have five houses they rent out to students in a northern university city. These have been bought over five years and are all financed on buy-to-let mortgages with decent deposits.

'We bought them as investments after I took early retirement from work and realised we would need additional income as a boost to our pensions,' says Roger. He works part-time in an enterprise agency as an advisor to small businesses and start-up ventures in the city.

Roger sees the tenants regularly as he collects the rent himself to keep costs down and keep an eye on his investments. In an area where good terraced housing is in good supply there is little scope for equity appreciation, but this is not why they made the investments, looking instead for good cash flow each month. The yields are good on such properties and students are well aware of the value of having a landlord who takes a keen interest in his tenants' well-being.

'The houses are each worth perhaps £30 000 to £45 000 and bring in rents of between £300 and £400 a month. This year we are looking to buy two more to give us a stronger portfolio in town. We have a good relationship with the university via the student accommodation office and would recommend this contact to other landlords.'

Their properties were all bought from estate agents, even though the city is one where the auction process is buoyant.

How it all works: the money stuff

The borrowing process

If you are using your own money it is still a gamble that you buy the right property for the best price and rent it out quickly to tenants who will stay put and pay the rent on time. If you are borrowing money from a commercial lender and repaying them plus interest will you recover all your costs and keep a house that hopefully rises in value? Or will you recover your costs of borrowing and also make a profit on the rental income? Should you ask for a commercial mortgage and be penalised for your honesty with a higher interest rate? Should you keep quiet about future tenants and ask for a personal domestic mortgage, knowing the bank could impose penalties if it learned about the tenants?

Questions, questions, questions. In this chapter we want to provide answers and information on some of the most frequently asked questions in property purchase. On the basis that 'forewarned is forearmed', you will be able to move through the process of buying an investment property with some sound knowledge that may save you time as well as money.

With the low yields on the stock market it is easy to understand why so many people are looking to property to be their financial salvation. Yet the risks are there too and we have to look at them, rather than be blinded by the potential to make a strong income. The popularity of buying to rent also means that people are jumping into the venture without knowing what the true score could be if things went wrong. They are ignorant of the simple things they should know about the process of buying their first investment property. Too many people making mistakes is of no benefit to the industry or to the individuals concerned.

With the current growth of the banking and lending sector, there has been an increase in the number and sophistication of the financial products on offer. The buy-to-let mortgage is one of these, and arguably makes it easier for you to become a landlord, with a financial instrument which openly tells us what it is for – to make a profit from rental of a house or flat. Originally devised by the Association of Residential Letting Agents and supported by mortgage lenders such as NatWest, Birmingham Midshires, Paragon Mortgages and Clydesdale Bank, it has made the investment in property far easier than just a few years ago.

If you are going to be borrowing for the purpose of buying to rent, the biggest challenge at the start will not be finding the right property but working out how to choose a mortgage that is right for you. There are hundreds of lenders offering thousands of options on mortgages. The array of repayment terms, borrowing criteria, interest rates, early redemption penalties, insurance premiums and earnings criteria can be mind-boggling.

You may have a view on interest rates and what they will do over the next three to five years, and this may lead your decision to go for a fixed-rate or a capped mortgage. You may have plans to develop your portfolio of properties and then move overseas – these factors could also influence the type and structure of the mortgage you opt for. You may not be borrowing in the conventional sense for buying to rent, and instead may find yourself taking equity from your main residence and using this as cash for either the deposit on an investment property or to buy the second property outright.

Meet the lenders

When you want to borrow money to buy the property look around, go and talk to a mortgage broker, ask colleagues if they know of an Independent Financial Adviser with whom you can discuss your mortgage. Alternatively, you can pick up one of the dedicated finance and mortgage magazines and run through their listings of mortgages. Consider that some of the best deals on your mortgage may come from the small, independent building societies. These are often focused on a traditional local market where they have provided simple finance for years. The best news about them is that due to their lack of spending on profile and promotion, they keep their overheads to a minimum and can offer low interest rates as a result.

Your high street bank will spend millions each year on the cost of promoting itself consistently and you will pay for this in your mortgage costs. On the other hand you may have banked with an organisation for anything between five years and 40 years and developed some loyalty through the relationship. In this time they have built up an accurate picture of you, your income and your savings patterns. Based on this intimate knowledge, they may be prepared to lend to you if you are on the edge of their criteria for borrowing when another lender who has never met you would be likely to turn you away. No one lender has the same exact criteria or approach to lending for property rental investments and you will be well advised to search around to find the best deal for you.

Borrowing for investment property

There are some criteria that are frequently demanded by lenders for buy-to-let property. The more enlightened are looking to make it as easy as possible for you to borrow money for a secure investment in property. It is in their interests to know that you have bought solid assets with your income and their lending generosity. If they were happy to lend you money to buy a car that depreciates the minute you drive it off the showroom forecourt, they will be doubly delighted to have helped you buy bricks and mortar. The bank considers this to be a better class of loan and the rate you are charged through the mortgage is obviously far less than for the car.

Lending guidelines

Each of the various lenders will have their own idea of what is considered a good or medium risk. Where some will lend for a minimum repayment term of ten years, others will seek a 15-year minimum. Some may want to see that your disposable income is in the order of 40 per cent of your net salary each month, others can be more or less generous. Either way, this is different from the usual approach to borrowing for your own principal residence where you can borrow two and a half to three times your income.

Remember that while you can get the funds to invest in your first property from many different lenders, they will not have common policies. By this I mean they have different criteria for the types of property they will let you buy. How flexible they will be can also differ enormously. The current spread of flexibility for helping you develop a small portfolio ranges from three to as many as ten investment properties.

The thinking with those who will extend the funds to help you buy five properties is usually grounded in two main reasons. The first is that if you are putting down a 20 per cent deposit per property, and you have a finite salary income each month from which five investment mortgages are deducted, you are left with little flexibility on salary

> The limiting of your borrowing to five properties is a reasonable attempt at prudence on the part of a lender.

day should things go wrong. The limiting of your borrowing to five properties is a reasonable attempt at prudence on the part of a lender.

The second is the simple assessment that by the time you have five flats or houses throwing off monthly rental income you should be able to cover your costs of mortgage and insurance, maintenance and annual service charges and still be able to declare a healthy profit on your use of the bank's money.

I know landlords who will buy five properties with one company to develop their starter portfolio and then expand using the positive cash flow into buying a few more houses without the use of a commercial mortgage. Once you have this fluidity, you should be able to repay some of the mortgages faster, either by increasing the repayments or by lump sum repayments.

Many lenders will be happy to let you pay off as much as 10 per cent of the loan each year through a straight repayment of the principal sum borrowed. This would be a good use of your improving cash flow from several properties.

Figure 9.1 summaries typical guidelines for mortgage lending against rental property (based on those of NatWest Mortgages in 2002). Remember that these can and will change.

Learning from the guidelines   Did you notice from the example in Fig. 9.1 that in this particular case the bank will consider lending money to a couple who are buying an investment property and who have a joint income as low as £20 000 a year, just £10 000 each person? If you ever hear people saying that they cannot afford to become a landlord, suggest they too read the small print in the lending criteria. On the other hand, you may choose to keep it as a secret.

Notice that this lender is looking to help you invest in a property where the gross rental is at least 150 per cent of the monthly mortgage costs. Others will go as low as 130 per cent. While the lower figure may sound good in that it allows you to finance a tighter operation, this also can put you into the trap of borrowing money for the dubious privilege of only just being able to cover your bills! Worth some deeper thought on your part perhaps.

Take care in completing the application

Something else to watch when you come to make your application for the mortgage funding, is the area of declaring your disposable income. In the example here the lender wants to see that your current expenses, including any existing mortgage, are covered by just 35 per cent of your basic income

Figure 9.1 Typical bank lending guidelines

The minimum term is 10 years

The maximum term for lending money is 25 years

The smallest loan is £15 000.

The highest property value accepted is £250 000

The maximum loan is 80 per cent of the valuation or purchase price of the property, whichever is lower (this reduces to 75 per cent for remortgages)

Income guidelines

Minimum annual income (single or joint) must be £20 000

The monthly rental income expected must be at least 150 per cent of the monthly mortgage repayment

Regular monthly outgoings (including any existing mortgage payments) must not be more than 35 per cent of monthly basic income before deductions

Scheme details

The administration fee is £200

New purchases and remortgages are accepted

Loans only provided for single assured shorthold tenancy agreements

Mortgage payments will be capital and interest

Fixed or variable rate mortgage

No mortgage guarantee indemnity (MGI) fee

The maximum number of mortgaged investment properties is four. This includes properties where the mortgage is with another lender

before deductions, such as tax and pension. In effect, if your salary is £2000 a month they are trying to see that your pre-allocated money exceeds no more than £700 per month. Have you understood this? In effect if you declare that you live on more than 35 per cent of your basic income you may be scoring an own-goal and disqualifying yourself from borrowing. Think this one through together before making a hasty application.

You want to borrow to invest and the lender wants you to. Yet if you complete an application saying in all honesty that you need 80 per cent of your income just to cover the existing bills and still have 20 per cent left, you may have just disqualified yourself – even if you can afford to take on the commitment of the additional mortgage.

There are ways around this. Consider putting down the most essential of costs such as existing mortgage, insurance, travel tickets, car running costs, food bills and utilities, and leaving the social expenses off the application. Not only are social expenses inexact, but they do not occur each month in the same proportion. If you are working hard to make your money work for you by investing in property, you will probably be looking to make savings in areas of casual spending anyway.

You might also look carefully at the way you incur expenses before you complete the application. Ensure that while you show you can afford the repayments on the property, you also make it clear that expenses are always met without trouble or default, even when the dry statistics and percentages of allowable borrowing falsely make it look as though you cannot afford to eat, let alone invest in your first investment property.

Last words on repaying the finances

Only borrow what you know you can repay yourself, and if you think the lender may have cause for questions or doubts, always add a written explanation to show how you will repay the loan, or details of other sources of income that will not necessarily show up clearly on the application form. Remember that you are also selling the lender on such things as how good a risk you are and how well you will look after or manage the property.

Mortgage application checklist

When you visit the lender for your application appointment it will yield dividends for you to take as much identification and paperwork as you can (see Fig. 9.2). The effort of collecting these papers together will allow the lender to tick the relevant boxes and process the application without any hold-ups.

In the space of a brief interview the lending officer for the bank or mortgage company will want to see plenty of evidence that you are who you claim to be. To echo the comment made before, see yourself as selling yourself and your reliability to repay the loan.

Hope for the self-employed investor

If you have been self-employed for more than ten years you are bound to be aware of the problems that used to exist around borrowing against the figures in your accounts. The trouble was that lenders took one look at the miniscule profits recorded by your accountant and then told you to come back when you had made some money! This was because the accountant would want you to be able to record every possible expense and show the smallest possible profit for your business – a practice which

Figure 9.2 Application checklist

Confirming your identity
Valid passport
Cheque guarantee card with photo ID
Marriage certificate
Full UK or EC driving licence
Employer's ID card
National insurance number
Medical card

Establishing your credit history
Council tax bill
Utility bills: electricity, water, gas
Telephone bill
Latest mortgage statement
Inland Revenue tax code statement
Contact details for your accountant (if you are self-employed)
Bank and credit card statements

Evidence of your financial details
Bank current account details (to set up direct debit instructions)
Last three payslips (for both of you if borrowing jointly)
Last three years of accounts (if you are self-employed)
Last P60
Rent book (if you have one)
Mortgage details
Monthly expenditure (work this out before you go)
Life insurance and pension details (latest statements)
Savings books
Investment plan and deposit account details

goes against the grain of a lender, who is seeking evidence of strong income before advancing any funds.

Things are much better today because credit guidelines have been relaxed and the approach to self-employed business owners particularly has become more lenient. This is not to say it is a walkover because the standard question from your intended lender is: 'Have you got three years of accounts to show us?' You may have started two and a half years ago and so may not be able to produce the full three years required, or you may have a very profitable business that is one year old and has no track record. Equally frustrating to you!

The number of lenders willing to deal specifically with the self-employed has grown but is still small, perhaps as few as one lender in ten have such a product. Those who will deal with you have taken the view that there should be little difference in the way an application is dealt with, whether it is for an employed person or the self-employed individual. Of course, if we look at who is the most tax efficient it will be the person with their own business almost every time.

Where you think you might have difficulty in proving that you can afford the investment mortgage, visit a mortgage broker and spend time with them. They will have a feel for the lending criteria of different organisations and are very likely to have good relationships with a few likely providers of the finance you want. Acting as a filter for the lender, the broker will work with you to get your application to be right for the funds. You don't pay the broker any money, as they get this from the lender as an introducer's fee.

Which mortgage for you?

While most investors opt for a repayment mortgage because it is easy to reconcile and also because the mortgage is normally paid off faster than a domestic mortgage, there are some who will still buy with an endowment mortgage. It may help to look at the two and see what they have to offer the potential investor.

In the case of a repayment mortgage, interest and capital are repaid over the course of the loan. Most early repayments cover the interest only but over time you begin to repay the capital too.

An endowment mortgage is linked to investments so that you make two payments each month. The larger monthly payment is to the lender for interest only. The second payment goes to an investment fund controlled by a life insurance company. Ideally, the money invested grows to become enough for you to repay the capital you borrowed. In reality however, many companies have had to declare the failure of endowment policies to repay sufficient capital to cover the debt. The product now has a poor profile for thousands of ordinary investors so do exercise care when considering your options.

Dealing with the interest   The interest on your loan can be repaid in a variety of ways.

- *The capped mortgage.* You have placed an upper limit on the monthly payments. When rates rise you will be protected against climbing costs of repayment. When they fall, you are secure that you have saved money already by being locked in at the capped rate.

- *Discount mortgage.* This rate gives you a percentage reduction on the variable rate for a limited time. While the discounted rate changes, just like variable rates, it is always a certain percentage below the base rate.
- *Fixed-rate mortgage.* You are buying in to a fixed repayment period of between one and five years. If interest rates rise, you hope you locked in at the right rate. If rates drop you may feel you are losing money.
- *Tracker mortgage.* Here you are paying the base rate and a fixed differential set by your lender. If the base rate were 5 per cent and the differential were to be 0.50 per cent, then the total rate would be 5.5 per cent.
- *Variable-rate mortgage.* Here you get to ride the yo-yo! When rates rise so do your payments, when they fall, your repayments also fall.

Having identified the above, you should note that most investors in property use either their own cash or a combination of cash deposit and repayment mortgage.

A common route is to put down cash, certainly on the smaller properties and then have them decorated and revalued by a lender, taking out a large mortgage of perhaps 80 per cent to create the cash for future purchases.

How the buying process works

Figure 9.3 shows briefly how the buying process works. Anyone who has bought a house will be familiar with most of this. What may be more unusual is buying at auction.

Buying at auction

'Exciting. Unnerving. Sure to get the adrenaline going.' A few ways of describing the atmosphere at a good auction where you can sometimes come away exhausted, particularly if you have bought a bargain property and managed to get it for a price very close to your original decision price.

An auction is always a place where you can expect the unexpected and marvel at the behaviour of people. At a recent auction of around 50 very ordinary residential and light industrial properties I saw 600 people turn up in the ballroom of a city centre hotel. Most of them looked as if they had not seen the catalogue in advance of the event and I was surprised at the number of babies and young children in the room. As the evening started and the bidding commenced I was surprised to see people get up and go after particular properties had been sold. Many had turned up just

Figure 9.3 Who does what and when

Your move	Their move
Decide where you want to invest and contact estate and letting agents	
Work with a lender to get 'in principle' agreement of mortgage	
Visit estate agents for suitable properties	
Have your solicitor ready to act as soon as you make an offer	
	Estate agent – Shows you selection of homes
Make an offer	
	Estate agent – Passes your offer to seller and it is accepted
Instruct the agent to take the property off the market that day	
Instruct solicitor to act for you	
	Solicitor – Calls seller's solicitor, requests title deeds and starts contract negotiations
Make formal mortgage application	
	Lender – Instructs a surveyor to do valuation of property
Request either short homebuyer's report or full building survey	
	Surveyor – Visits the property and writes report
	Lender – Accepts the valuation and proceeds with the loan
Receive surveyor's report and decide to proceed	
Instruct letting agent to find tenants	
	Letting agent – Sends agreement
Arrange for buildings insurance if freehold. To start on exchange of contracts	
	Solicitor – Begins searches. Checks inclusion of fixtures and fittings as well as alterations
	Solicitor – Checks mortgage details with lender and contract details with seller's solicitor
Pay deposit of 10 per cent of purchase price. This is held by your solicitor until exchange date	

Figure 9.3 (continued)

Your move	Their move
	Solicitor – Exchanges signed contracts with seller's solicitor. Transfers the deposit amount. If you pull out now you lose your deposit
	Solicitor – Asks the lender to have funds available for completion
	Solicitor – Makes final searches
	Solicitor – Prepares transfer deed, signed by you and held by seller's solicitor until completion
Request that bank be ready to transfer any funds other than mortgage amount	
	Letting agent – Credit checks and references for tenants
	Lender – Transfers monies to your solicitor's account prior to completion
	Solicitor – Transfers the final balance to seller's solicitor on completion date. Receives transfer deed, keys and Land Registry certificate
You now own the property and instruct gas and electricity testing team to act	
Arrange contents insurance	
	Solicitor – Transfer deed is stamped, Stamp Duty paid and deed sent to Land Registry recording you as the new owner
	Letting agent – Receives gas safety certificate and confirms moving in date of tenants
	Solicitor – Title deed sent to lender as security on loan
	Solicitor – Sends you bill for work done
	Letting agent – Tenants pay deposit and first month's rent, and collect keys
Receive first rent minus letting agent's fees. Congratulations!	

to see the price that a neighbouring house would fetch under the hammer. Once they knew the worth of their own, they went home.

Why people sell at auction   If you have a property that you must sell to realise the money quickly, then putting it up for auction may be the most reliable way to achieve your goal. A building society, with property that has been repossessed after a default by the original borrower of one of their mortgages, will sell the property at auction for a variety of reasons. These include the best practice reason of being seen to attempt to get the best price possible for it.

Other properties that seem to be sold predominantly at auction are those which seem difficult to value. These can include residential property with sitting tenants and a peppercorn rental income, as well as properties requiring much repair work, and portfolios of investment property generally.

Why you can't bid by accident   When you are new to the auction process, consider using a specialist with local knowledge. Steven Sykes of Sands Property Search says: 'Don't fall for the joke that says you can leave an auction with a house in your name simply because you smoothed your hair or waved a fly away from your face. This looks good in a comedy script, but auctioneers are skilled readers of crowds and they know when they are making a sale that it is to someone who actually knows they are bidding. Because the audience of people attending auctions has changed greatly over recent years, most auctioneers will take a moment at the start of the event just to remind people to make clear bids and to reassure them that they will be asked repeatedly if their bid is a true bid.'

In the introduction, the auctioneer will probably announce that there will be a recording of all bids by a steward moving among the audience; that the properties are being sold under certain conditions, such as 'all being sold freehold and in vacant possession'; and that the properties in question are being sold under the auctioneer's general conditions of sale.

When the final bid in a round of bidding is announced, you may hear the auctioneer shout something along the lines of: 'Not quite enough, if the bidders would like to come forward after the sale.' This is the moment you learn that the price finally reached is close to or just below the reserve price. Because it was so close, the auctioneer continued accepting bids. When the bidder speaks to the stewards of the auction he or she will be told how close the bid was to the requested price from the vendor. In this instance the auctioneer's team will call the vendor and ask if they are prepared to accept the bid. In the event that they accept, the paperwork goes ahead. If the vendor seeks a better offer, a member of the team may liaise between bidder and vendor on the telephone so that with a few hundred or a few thousand pounds more, the sale can go ahead on the same day.

At the fall of the hammer there is a legal obligation to purchase the property so you will need to go to the event with your cheque book and the finance for the property available to draw upon within a few days of the event.

Read the catalogue for clues   The seller or seller's agent will be listed against each item. Where it says 'For sale by mortgagee in possession' you know you are about to bid for a repossessed property. In the same description of the seller, the catalogue will tell you if it is a solicitor or perhaps a lending institution. Buying repossessions is a sensible strategy because as a general rule these will be listed at about 20 per cent less than market value locking in immediate value.

It is also worth looking for the address of the solicitors acting for the vendor. If the vendor is in Essex and you are bidding for the property in Cardiff, there is a good chance the property is being sold as part of an estate, with the proceeds being awaited, in this case, by the family in Essex. When people inherit property they will often look to sell it as quickly as possible. Either the distance or the memories associated with the place mean they have no interest in the house. In their haste to receive the proceeds, the property can often be priced for a quick sale.

Figure 9.4 shows some samples from a catalogue. With Lot 35, the fact that it has been recently improved means you should be able to let it quickly. However, you will still need to check the standard of the work before bidding for this. Notice that the vendor's solicitor is a long way from here and you can probably assume they will accept the first quick offer. In fact, £10 000 or £11 000 would probably be accepted before the property goes to auction. There are many houses like this in the area but the property should be worth £18 000 to £20 000 the minute it is yours.

The tied-together properties in Lot 36 beat the reserve. They sold for £70 000, including the house and two light industrial units totalling more than 2500 sq ft of rentable business premises. The annual rent on the two units would be about £5000 each and the house would bring in £400 a month. So, after a few minutes bidding you have three properties and a rent roll of £15 000, about 20 per cent of your money a year.

Look for value   Low prices at auction inevitably mean spending more money on renovation and maintenance once the property is yours. If you need to do the work yourself you will save money on labour paid to others, but you may lose as much as a month's rent if it takes you longer

Figure 9.4 Samples from an auction catalogue

Lot 35
Address of the property: *****

Description: Traditional two-bedroom mid-terrace house recently improved and ideal and ready for letting. Convenient for town centre.

Accommodation: **Ground floor**. Through living-room, kitchen, bathroom.
First Floor. Two bedrooms. Outside: **Rear yard**.

Vendor's solicitors: in a town 200 miles away.

Guide price: £10 000 to £15 000

Lot 36
Address of the property: *****

Description: A two-bedroom, brick & tile house, estimated to have been constructed circa 1955 requiring some modernisation and improvement. Offered for sale on behalf of the mortgagee in possession and trustee in bankruptcy. **Please note**: This lot and two others will initially be offered as one lot with a guide price of £50,000 plus. If the properties fail to reach the reserve price they will then be offered individually.

Accommodation: **Ground floor.** Hall leading to living room, kitchen, bathroom with separate wc. **First Floor**: 2 bedrooms. **Outside**: lean-to conservatory/store, small rear yard and large front forecourted garden

to do the work. A parking space would make a property worth more. Look at what might give extra value, such as wooden floors, original fireplaces and other features such as an attractive yard or back garden.

About a week before the auction, the vendor's solicitor will provide the auctioneer with a documentation pack aimed at hastening the sale process. This pack will contain the local search results and the contract of sale. You should either inspect this documentation yourself or employ a local solicitor to do the checks for you.

The vendor will not provide a building survey and you should arrange for this yourself if you consider the property worth your investment.

After the hammer goes down!   Have your cheque book with you at the event because you will be required to hand over a 10 per cent deposit. You must also be in a position to complete on the property within 28 days of the sale. At the back of the auction catalogue you will find the 'general conditions of sale'. These outline the process, responsibilities and obligations of the auctioneer, vendor and buyer of the property and will give you insight into the broader process. These typically include the following:

- Each purchaser shall be deemed to purchase with full knowledge of all the conditions subject to which the property is sold.

- If a person attending the sale intends to bid on behalf of some other person or company, he shall, before the sale commences, hand the auctioneer a note of the name and address of that person or company, failing which, the auctioneer shall be entitled to treat the bidder as the contractual purchaser whether or not the auction contract was signed for or on behalf of some other person or company.

- On each lot being knocked down the successful bidder must provide the auctioneer's clerk with his name and address details, or those of the person for whom he has been bidding.

- All bids are to be made clearly. The auctioneer reserves the right to regulate bidding and to refuse undesirable bids. The vendor reserves the right to bid up to the reserve price or to authorise the auctioneer to do so. Each lot is offered subject to a reserve price being reached. In the event of a dispute it is the auctioneer who has the final word.

- If the deposit cheque used fails to clear, then the vendor can offer the property for resale and still has recourse to claim damages from the bidder who was successful.

- The purchaser shall be deemed to have made local land charge searches and prudent enquiries of the relevant local authorities and other parties, and to have satisfied themselves about the status of all such issues.

- The property is believed to have been correctly described with approximate measurements in the catalogue. In the event of a mis-description the auctioneer cannot be held liable.

- The auctioneers reserve the right to sell the property prior to auction.

- The vendor reserves the right to alter or add to the particulars and conditions of sale at any time prior to the sale.

- Nothing contained within the catalogue can or should be taken as a warranty by the vendor or the auctioneers that the property is authorised under any planning acts, leases or otherwise for use for any specific purposes.

- The purchase of the property by the buyer is the responsibility of the buyer who should ensure that all relevant searches have been made.

- The purchaser needs to be satisfied that the particulars of sale are accurate.

- The purchaser admits to have: inspected the property, obtained professional advice, and made the decision to buy independently of any other party.

- Each bidder needs to understand that he or she is personally liable on making the offer.

- The successful bidder is under a binding contract at the time of sale and from this point the insurance of the building is the responsibility of the purchaser.

- The successful bidder will pay a 10 per cent or a lump sum amount and sign a contract before leaving the auction room.

Basic auction rules Give your self plenty of time to attend the auction. Try to arrive a full hour before the advertised time. Once there, stay at the back of the room so you can size up the competition and act once you sense the bidding slow down on the property you want.

Preparation is essential before you get there. Be clear which property you want, have a maximum offer and stick to it.

Don't be tempted to bid for a property as a second best option if you have not done the homework on it.

Don't go more than £1000 or perhaps 5 per cent over the price you told yourself you would bid at.

If you don't get the house you wanted at the price you decided, remember that another similar property will be there at the next auction.

> If you don't get the house you wanted at the price you decided, remember that another similar property will be there at the next auction.

The cost of buying a house

Have you forgotten that buying your own first home was an expensive exercise? To want to do the same thing again and for other people, namely your tenants, must surely be against all the odds. Interest rates could rise so that your mortgage costs could be greater than your rental income. Your tenant could stop paying the rent and refuse to leave the property, forcing you into costly and messy legal action. Tenants in a housing block where you have a flat could pressure the management committee into repricing the charges and fees downwards, leaving you with more responsibilities and costs for maintenance and redecorations.

Don't underestimate the true cost of getting started as a landlord.

Alastair Kennedy of Howsons Accountants in Leek says: 'Too many investors ignore or forget the extra costs associated with the purchase of the property until it is too late to stop. Aside from the stamp duty, solicitors' charges, search fees and the actual mortgage, what about the bills you will face for renovation, redecoration and maintenance of the property? On top of this you must plan and budget for the inevitable empty periods when the house is without tenants. Are you prepared for this and can you afford to face such potential challenges?'

Buying a property

Figure 9.5 outlines some of the minimum charges and costs you are likely to incur when buying properties for your investment portfolio. Regardless of the size and purchase price of the property you opt for there are many costs which stay virtually the same throughout the purchase process. Others vary according to the value or the size of the property.

Figure 9.5 makes several assumptions:

■ Properties are in reasonable condition and only need minor decoration of some of the rooms.

■ Wiring is safe and that minor adjustments may need doing, such as adding sockets or more power to the kitchen.

■ Kitchens and bathrooms may need new fittings or cabinets.

■ Rents on the three properties are £400, £600 and £800 a month.

■ The finder's fee for getting tenants is 10 per cent of the rent or a minimum of £200.

■ That a finder's fee *or* full management fee is charged at start of tenancy.

Stamp duty   Stamp duty is paid to the Inland Revenue on the purchase of all properties over £60 000. It is an indirect tax on property ownership. Each year, it is the topic of debate just before the announcement of the Chancellor's latest Budget.

Property up to £59 999	No stamp duty to pay
Property from £60 000 – £250 000	1 per cent
Property from £250 001 – £500 000	3 per cent
Property over £500 001	4 per cent

This can be a lot of money to find over and above the purchase price and there have been some inventive ways of keeping the stamp duty to the

Figure 9.5 Charges and costs

Buying	£25 000 property	£50 000 property	£100 000 property	Estimated spending	Actual spending
Searches	£50–£150	£50–£150	£50–£150		
Land Registry	£80	£80	£80		
Lender's legal fees	£300	£300	£300		
Lender's valuation	£125	£125	£175		
Survey fee	£150	£250	£400		
Buildings insurance	£150	£200	£200		
Mortgage indemnity guarantee	£250	£500	£1 200		
Solicitor disbursements	£50	£50	£50		
Solicitor's fees	£350	£500	£900		
Stamp duty	Nil	Nil	£1 000		
Decorating					
Painting	£600	£850	£1 200		
Electrical and plumbing	£1000	£1 500	£2 500		
Simple furnishing and fittings	£1000	£2500	£3 500		
Safety certificates	£100	£125	£150		
Letting fees					
Finding tenants and letting only	£200	£200	£200		
Or full management @ 15%	£60	£90	£120		
Tenancy agreement	£100	£100	£100		
Inventory service	£60	£60	£60		
Estimated minimum costs	**£4125**	**£7280**	**£11 985**		

lowest scale. If you are buying a property that is for sale at £255 000 is there a way you can bid £249 000 for the house and pay a separate £6000 for the curtains, carpets and contents? The £7650 you would have had to pay on a property at £255 000 becomes £2490 at the 1 per cent rate of duty. A saving of £5160. Be imaginative but don't push it too far. The Inland Revenue takes a dim view of the deliberate avoidance of chargeable tax.

New to the world of business? The worries over the number of newcomers to the buying to rent market has led to The Association of Residential Letting Agents (ARLA) calling for the training of landlords before they can rent out investment property. Insurance bodies and bank lenders have also been keen to see the introduction of strong checks on the level of insurance cover would-be landlords have against redundancy and the loss of their own main incomes. Make contact with the association and ask about some of its initiatives as well as getting the opportunity to attend useful regional meetings.

Another little set of initials that you have either forgotten since you bought your own home, or you have never heard before, is MIG. You will discover many such abbreviations as you go through the mortgage application process. MIG stands for Mortgage Indemnity Guarantee and is yet another charge for you to pay. Other names for it might be MIP (Mortgage Indemnity Premium) or IGP (Indemnity Guarantee Premium). Insurance cover such as this is charged when your borrowing is greater than 75 per cent of the purchase price of a property. This once-only payment protects your lender in case you default on the loan. The higher the percentage of the property's value you borrow, the greater the rate you pay for this cover. But, even where the bank gets their money back the insurance company can still come after you for the value of their payout to the bank!

Other insurance you should consider is for the ongoing payment of rental income. Several companies can provide this, giving some peace of mind when you are faced with a lengthy void period i.e. without tenants.

LANDLORDS TALKING – SUSAN

Susan lives with her partner and owns a property in a nearby coastal town. It is a terraced house occupied by a tenant on benefit. They bought the place 14 years ago and it has not appreciated as much as they had hoped in that time. The mortgage is a standard one, and the lender knows there is a tenant in the property.

Susan and her partner had thought it sensible to have an investment property and so bought in a town they could afford. With hindsight, they would have done a lot differently and say they would have stayed with working tenants only. To save costs they manage the property themselves, visiting every couple of years.

'Our current tenant of about 12 years' standing is on benefit. He is a Dickensian character and a delightful but compulsive liar. We had a period when he promised to send money, would even ring up and say it was on its way, and it didn't come. My partner found this very stressful and in the past we have had to resort to some heavy tactics just to get the rent paid. Our very first tenants were a delightful couple but were only there for about 18 months.'

'If there were a realistic prospect of buying further property we would select somewhere with greater potential for capital growth, giving us more opportunity to support my sons. On balance it has been a good investment and gone very well,' says Susan, who reads the press for news and articles as she considers another property.

Meet the professionals

Throughout the property buying process you will be dealing with specialists whose job it is to provide information, guidance and help. Reviews are mixed on the benefits of the different parties, yet buying property cannot be done without them. It makes sense to understand their roles and know more about the ways they are supposed to be useful.

Working with an accountant

Worth his or her weight in gold, your accountant needs to understand your financial goals as well as your financial circumstances. Although a rarely mentioned professional in buying property, I start with accountants because of the disproportionate value they bring to the process. Although you may not consider having an accountant if you are receiving a salary or a pension and buying property with the income you receive, it is worth reconsidering as soon as you have three or four houses in your portfolio. They will be there to ensure that you pay your true taxes to the Inland Revenue, but not before you have claimed all the relevant and allowable expenses.

You are liable to pay tax on any rental income you receive from your property and yet there are a good number of allowances you can claim before computing the final tax figure. You can deduct the cost of the interest payments on your mortgage, the cost of the letting agents, property maintenance and also an amount for wear and tear if your property is furnished.

Taking advantage of costs and expenses

You should record all costs incurred in setting up a property business because the accountant may not regard them as eligible to be claimed if you cannot provide receipts. If the business is a full-time venture, you would be able to claim the costs of running the business, such as the use of an office, furniture, heating, lighting and stationery.

However, let's not run before we can walk. You are starting with the purchase of your first investment property and the creation of a cash flow.

Using your personal allowance   You can offset the tax to be paid on your earnings in a number of ways. The first of these is the use of your personal tax allowance which, in 2002, stands at £4500. This means that you can earn £4500 before paying tax on your earnings. Over and above this amount you will pay tax on the difference. If you buy a property with your partner and they are not making use of their personal allowance because they are not working, the rental income tax liabilities can be offset significantly if the property is in joint names.

Claiming expenses   You can also claim various expenses that you incur. The interest you pay on the mortgage to buy the property is a deduction, as are repair and maintenance bills. The cost of furniture bought expressly for the property is allowed and items such as carpets, the shower curtain, kitchen accessories, crockery and cutlery are all legitimate costs. When you make trips to the property to decorate it, incur the expense of an electrician or a decorator, you can claim this cost. When you have a building rewired or a kitchen fitted, again, keep the paperwork and claim it as an expense incurred necessarily in the management of the property. If I visit a town to go and discuss the tenants of a house, then I will claim the travel costs, the related phone calls and other logistics of arranging the visit. The bill you are presented with by your accountant is also something you can use to offset the potential tax bill raised on your rental and other business incomes.

As with any use of a professional adviser, it is prudent to make detailed notes of your income and expenditure. The accountant will have a preferred method of keeping records. For many landlords who are in full-time employment, it will be sufficient to enter the records of all earned rental income on a self-assessment tax form. However, for those who already have business interests it is more likely that rental income will be declared elsewhere. Where this is the case you might produce accounts using either a paper-based or an electronic format such as Sage or Quickbooks. The best rule? If in doubt, keep it simple. You must be able to keep your own records and the best system or method of doing so is the one that you are the most comfortable with.

The rent-a-room scheme   One of the ways to raise money from property is through this scheme where you can rent a room or rooms in your house. Intended as a way of having more people stay in owner-occupied property, the scheme has been very successful. Provided the income you receive on this is less than £4250 each year, it is tax-free.

Working with a solicitor

Despite being crucial to the process because of the intricacies of law and the transfer of ownership of a property into your possession, the solicitor will appear sometimes to be remote. Even when at their busiest they can give the impression that nothing is happening. Your greatest frustration will probably be expressed towards your solicitor because the slow pace of transferring documents or funds can be infuriating.

The specialist knowledge they possess means that solicitors cannot be bypassed, but you should select one because they can do the work effectively. If the practice does not focus on conveyancing, then find a new solicitor. If you are half way through your first meeting with a solicitor and you don't feel confident with the responses you are getting, you are quite within your rights to shop elsewhere. Asking around among other families who have bought investment property is a good way to identify helpful solicitors, as well as discussions with the local estate agents.

Questions to ask a solicitor include:

- Do they specialise in conveyancing?
- How quickly can they carry out local authority searches?
- Have they confirmed what they will do and what their fees will be?
- Do they have much experience of working with investors?
- Do they promise to be accessible or to return calls promptly?

Working with an estate agent

Love them or hate them, if you are looking to buy property from a seller through what is called the 'private treaty sale' route, the estate agent will be the intermediary. The exception to this is through auctions where the seller sets a target price, which is known as the reserve (*see* Chapter 9).

Your estate agent should be the sort of person who will ring you with advance notice of suitable properties and who will work with you to help you

> Your estate agent should be the sort of person who will ring you with advance notice of suitable properties.

develop a portfolio. Often a good source of introduction to finance, you will again need to remember that the lender will pay them an introducer's fee for having passed you on to the financial intermediary.

The estate agent is working on behalf of the seller or vendor and it is their job to get the maximum price possible for a property. This is true whether they are selling for the vendor or for the mortgagee in possession, usually the mortgage company which has repossessed a property after someone failed to pay their mortgage.

When working with an estate agent:

- Be clear with them about your budget.

- If you know that good property can be bought for £40 000–50 000 in that area, don't let them fob you off with £80 000–90 000 property details.

- Tell them exactly what level of return you are looking for on an investment.

- Find out how long they have been established in the area.

- Ask about other investment properties they have sold recently.

- Ask them if they invest in rental property themselves.

- Do you feel confident that they understand and also appreciate your needs?

- Ask them if they have a property rental and management team in-house.

Working with a financial adviser

In Chapter 9, which covered mortgage finance and the amount of borrowing you might consider right against the value of each investment property, I was focusing on helping you to consider what might be a good return on your investment. Part of this involved looking at how much you felt it was either comfortable or sensible to look at borrowing.

Most of us will probably look first to our bank or building society when it comes to thinking about a second mortgage or a buy-to-let mortgage. Yet if we do this we limit ourselves as to the full potential of what is available in the financial markets. Most of the banks and building societies are tied to their own products for which they are seeking the best financial return. This means their ability to offer you the product which is the most suited to you, is either unlikely, or not in their interests. This is hardly the best position to be in when trying to identify the best mortgage instrument for your own private and personal circumstances. For this reason I suggest you might want to investigate using an independent financial adviser (IFA).

Regardless of whether you are looking for an investment mortgage or the life assurance to provide you with cover for it, or perhaps some other investment programmes which you think might be a good place to invest some of your profits from rental income, there is a good product out there. This will be the product that is right for you.

With so many mortgages available and many types of supporting life cover available, you are potentially entering a minefield and you will need someone to help you negotiate the best and the safest way through. Only an IFA can provide you with unbiased, expert advice and access to the widest range of products.

What an IFA will do

An IFA is a professional person, dedicated to the provision of high-quality, unbiased financial advice. Given that there are thousands of financial products in the marketplace, being an IFA is a full-time commitment, requiring that they undergo thorough training and examinations before they are allowed to provide any advice to clients.

Instead of being tied to the products of one company, IFAs are bound to the law. This requires them to give advice that is most closely suited to your personal requirements. This will most likely be based upon product factors such as charges, flexibility, performance, service, and levels of risk and security. This means that an IFA will look to the market for the right product from one angle only – what is best for you. Many good buy-to-let lenders will only sell their products through IFAs acting as their intermediaries so check that your IFA writes a lot of mortgage business. Many IFAs have little understanding of the landlord/investor market at all and you want one who knows and understands the buy-to-let industry.

Each IFA has to be regulated by a recognised authority and is obliged therefore to give only 'suitable advice'. This again relates back to them having to have a full understanding and awareness of your requirements and circumstances before they help you choose a financial product.

Once an IFA has recommended a product to you, they must provide you in writing with the reasons why they consider this to be the case. This serves to ensure you are fully informed before you commit yourself to anything.

What qualifications does an IFA have? The benchmark qualification for an IFA is the Financial Planning Certificate (FPC), and for an adviser to be considered competent they must hold all three components of this certificate or the equivalent. There will also be some advisers who have advanced qualifications in a specialist area, for example, mortgages or life assurance.

> There will also be some advisers who have advanced qualifications in a specialist area, for example, mortgages or life assurance.

How does an IFA get paid? There are two ways IFAs are paid. The first is the most common and relates to the commission paid to the adviser from the company whose product you have invested in. You will not be charged any extra and it is usual for the adviser to tell you in advance about the commission he or she will be paid by the finance company based on the product recommendation.

The second route is for you to pay your IFA on the basis of time spent in advising you. This will usually be an hourly rate. In the case of fee-based advice, when you select to buy a product, such as a mortgage, then any commission which is built into the product is normally rebated to you (either as a cost reduction or as extra money which can be invested in your product).

Finding a financial adviser

The best route for this is to make contact with the IFA promotion hotline listed in the resources section. Otherwise keep a lookout for the IFA logo in adverts and on literature, as well as in the high street.

While it is not crucial that you become best friends with your IFA, if it is difficult for you to either trust or to feel comfortable with an IFA you meet, then I am hardly going to recommend you stay with them. Instead, exercise your right to meet some others until you feel you are getting best advice from someone you can relate to.

Working with a letting agent

The letting and management agent has two levels of support for you as a landlord. In the first the agent will simply find suitable tenants, set up a tenancy agreement to rent the property and take the first month's rent and a deposit. For many private landlords this is exactly what they want from their agent and nothing further.

The second service level is one of carrying out regular checks on the house and passing the rent to you at the end of each month. They can also find other suppliers for decorating, renovation, gardening, window cleaning, internal cleaning, and so on, as you consider necessary.

The rates for the two roles differ greatly and you should expect to pay

10 per cent for the finding service and around 15 per cent for the full management of the property. This second rate can seem expensive, until you consider the time you would have to spend in seeing to each and every request of a difficult tenant, taking time away from your work or interests just to be on the site for a few minutes.

Generally speaking, landlords will use the full management service where they consider the use of their time better placed elsewhere. Landlords who live close to their properties may tend to use the tenant finding service and then keep contact with the tenants through regular visits. The difficulty here is that you can become too keen to get on well with a tenant, and once this cosy relationship is established a tenant may manipulate you into doing things that an agent would know are the tenant's responsibility.

Most of the larger estate agency groups have letting and management teams in their branches. Some of these businesses will be members of ARLA (the Association of Residential Letting Agents) and others will not. Instead they may be members of the NAEA (National Association of Estate Agents) and offer an equally good service for landlords. Membership of these associations gives you a sense that you are well represented because the companies have signed up to a code of professional conduct and behaviour.

Where the agent is a part of a larger estate agency practice it can be useful to foster a good relationship. This is because the agent will be aware of properties coming up for sale, either by private treaty or through auction, and can provide you with an early opportunity to gain more information. This could be through access to an early inspection of a property, or the early receipt of auction particulars.

When working with a letting agent:

- Be sure they understand your level of ambition as a landlord.
- Establish a rapport with the individuals of the letting team.
- As you develop a larger portfolio ask for a discount on their fee rates.
- Let them know what sort of a landlord you are; are you in it for the long-term or the short-term?
- Make your strategy clear to them and say what type of tenants you want to provide for.

A final few words

When you make your first buy-to-rent investment the number of names you will hear can be overwhelming. Friends and colleagues will each recommend banks, solicitors and advisers to you. You are expected to make intelligent and informed decisions when you have little or no knowledge. Instead of taking the first name you hear, do a little research. Visit the broker or the adviser who is recommended. Ask for introductions to a few of their existing buy-to-rent clients. Do your homework again.

As you develop a small portfolio you will begin to hear fewer names recommended by a broader group of investors. These are most likely to be the names of good professionals that you can begin to work with yourself. Remember that the amount of time and effort they can save you through their own knowledge and contacts is worth paying for and worth having access to. Look after the small band of professionals you gather around you and they will respond quickly to your requests for further help and investment.

LANDLORDS TALKING – TONY

Tony is a shopkeeper who has built up a strong portfolio of 23 rented properties. All in one town, his properties are either two-bed terraced houses or houses split into small flats or bedsit.

'I have never used a letting agent and collect the rent myself where I need to. Otherwise it is paid directly to the bank by the tenants. Someone works with me part-time to check the rents have been paid because I am dyslexic and could not manage that job myself,' says Tony.

'The money from the properties is very useful, but I still consider my main activity to be a retailer and shopkeeper. The rent money is something extra. I always wanted to have a few houses so my boy could choose whether to work in the shops with me or try his hand in a different business.' Most of the properties are owned outright, with just three having mortgage finance attached to them.

'My favourite tenants are the ones on housing benefit. Most of them seem grateful for a good landlord and the beauty for me is that they can stay so long in the property. I have had several tenants more than four years, and one person has been renting a house for eight years with the money paid like clockwork every single week.'

His one regret is collecting the rent for so long himself, and he is 'looking at giving this work to a letting agent in exchange for a much-discounted rate. This will be a flat fee per property rather than a straight percentage.'

Building your portfolio

First, I am bound to say that you must fall in love with property if you are ever to go beyond the one property. Whatever your stance on risk, whether you are a softly, softly person or you love to live out there on the edge, you will only buy a second and then a third property if you can see that the experience will not be a nightmare. Walking through the front door into an empty terraced house or climbing the stairs to look at a second-floor flat may not have you jumping up and down with happiness – because there are always plenty more properties to see – but hopefully you will not be numb at the prospect. Many professional landlords and investors tell me they love the 'chase' for the next property, for the feeling it gives them. This positive sense of being stems from doing something they love and are comfortable with.

If you get the same thrill from completing on your first investment property as you did when buying the home you live in, then I would hazard a guess and say you will enjoy developing a small portfolio of at least half a dozen properties. This number is usually sufficient for you to have been able to receive enough rental income after costs that you could manage to survive on the revenue in the event that you lost your job or decided to walk away from it.

By this stage it doesn't really matter where the properties are for them to give you a liveable income. Six properties in an area of low to modest incomes and rented at £300 to £600 per month provide you with a very decent £1800 to £3600 each month. Six properties that are perhaps in slightly different locations and throwing off gross rent of £600 to £1000 a month provide you with a figure of £3600 to £6000. Surely this would be a helpful sum to have in either the background or the foreground depending on your viewpoint!

> It doesn't really matter where the properties are for them to give you a liveable income.

We started the book with a look at the lifestyle benefits of having your own cash flow from property rental and I would ask you to reconsider these goals again now. With an income that provides you with sufficient revenue to at least match your current work income, take the time to picture the options now available to you.

It's payback time!

No! Not a line from a bad film, but the way that professional investors will assess the benefits and the return of a particular property. You can see this rule being applied by investors when they are at auctions or when going through property details with an estate agent. They want to know how long they have to wait before the house has paid for itself.

An investing friend will look at a house, perhaps a three-bedroom property in a large town, and consider the potential rent. Will it bring in £600 a month? That is £7200 a year. If the property is valued at £60 000 then the gross rent is enough to pay the value of the house in just over eight years. If the same size property were to be for sale at £50 000 and the rent stays the same, all of a sudden the payback period is down to seven years and looking more attractive. If the original £60 000 house can be rented out at £800 a month or £9600 a year, then the payback becomes slightly over six years. Using a simple process like this gives you a tool with which to judge your potential return on a property.

This is important given that most professional investors in residential property invest first for the cash flow that it provides and secondly for any potential capital growth. Most rental property will never experience huge price increases but will give steady returns.

London is a law unto itself in terms of the growth in property values relative to original purchase prices. Many friends have struggled in London to buy their first property and experienced the rewards of big property price hikes that have given them great capital growth.

If this is important for you then do consider investing in more highly priced communities where the scope for growth in property value over a few years, say five or six, is part of your intention when buying the property.

Figure 11.1 shows how to calculate the payback time, ignoring any costs and capital growth.

Houses versus flats

Right at the outset and with your very first property investment in mind, will you go for a flat or for a house? The scope for each type is different as are the rules to be considered when making your choice.

Figure 11.1   Calculating the payback period

Property price e.g. £100 000	Divided by ÷	Annual rental £12 000	Equals =	Payback time 8 years+

Every investor I know has their own favourites. For me, the money has to be on traditional Victorian terraced homes. Wherever they are, the build quality is good and they are tough enough to withstand virtually any treatment from tenants or neighbours. The more traditional the community the longer the tenants stay. This works out well because although rentals in such areas can be lower, the empty periods without tenants are far less.

There are other benefits to the neighbourhood. Where families have lived there for years and people know each other's business, it can make it easier for you to find a tenant who moves in because their aunty or their parents live nearby and their place of work is within 20 minutes. Word travels fast that your property will be available and the grapevine effect means that someone learns about the house to rent just as you are ready for a new tenant, often before!

For my friend Paul and his family, they have always preferred two and three-bedroom apartments in purpose-built blocks, always close to a Tube station in central London. Not only have they received good rental income for the proximity of the flats to the City and the West End, but also the capital value of their properties has increased enormously and with welcome regularity. Something they have in common with many landlords who like to buy properties in established blocks is the feeling that you may as well stick with what you know and buy more of a good thing through further investments in that same block.

I enjoy strong income from a property I bought years ago when first working in London. It is a maisonette or two-storey flat in a block of 20 such properties and was bought from a couple who had lived there as council tenants for many years before they exercised their option under a 'right to buy' scheme in the late 1980s. The property is close to public transport and a great place to live for young professionals on starting salaries for a year or so while they get to know London and before they can afford to buy a place of their own. I bought it in exactly the same circumstances and most tenants have been in the same category, moving out because their incomes have risen and they want to get a property they can call 'home'.

However, blocks of apartments or flats can have unique problems that have always put me off owning more than one in the same block. The first of these is the leasehold status of most such blocks, meaning that you only have your leasehold share of the property for a set number of years, after which the property is no longer yours and reverts back to the freeholder. Resident committees and the potential for expensive charges levied by the management company for maintenance, repairs or redecoration have never appealed. On the other hand, you might find it comforting to know a building well. This may provide you with a certain feeling of security, enough to give you the confidence to buy other investment apartments in the same block. The positive is that you can keep an eye on the general building and it may feel good to live close to the investment.

> Blocks of apartments or flats can have unique problems that have always put me off owning more than one in the same block.

My preference for houses is undoubtedly helped by the knowledge that the freehold is mine and that there are no committees to fight with. While many landlords do say that a house can be empty for longer than a flat (on the basis that houses are further away from busy town centres where the flats tend to be) others will quote their returns on the houses as greater due to the increase in house prices being steeper than that for flats and apartments.

Figure 11.2 summarises the arguments.

Figure 11.2 The house versus flat debate

House	Flat
Freehold	Leasehold
Greater potential for good increase in value	Steady growth in value
Steady rental income	High rental returns
Payback generally longer than flats	Fast payback period
Broad options for tenant groups	Enjoyed by professionals
	Management company fees
	Resident committee
	Building maintenance bills

Who are your tenants?

One of the deciding factors over houses or flats is bound to be the tenant group you think you will be focusing on. Not only will this affect the types of property you invest in, it will also affect the returns you make.

Students If you are looking at the student market where three or four people want to share a property, they will naturally be looking for a house. They will be expecting to find what they want within a mile or so of the campus to get in and out of college quickly and without any complicated use of public transport. In any university town the best place to start to learn the local situation will be the university accommodation office.

Working professionals In an urban centre, busy professionals will most likely have little spare time and have little interest in gardening. For these people the attraction of a flat is that they can come in, close the door, and be alone within a larger community of residents. With their higher incomes and the demand for housing close to city centres, there is every chance you will reap a higher return on the flat than the house.

Single-parent families Another important group of tenants are single-parent families who often want a combination of space and security. A garden may be important for children to be able to play and run around in and the parent may want to feel safe in an area where there is a sense of community and belonging. While you can ensure that there is a sense of security within the home you provide and you control the outside space by choosing the types of property you invest in, the community issue is one you have slightly less control of.

The retired person People who have finished their working careers may have steady pensions and are looking for a place to enjoy. They may have sold on their former family home and have good savings, or perhaps they have chosen to move closer to children and grandchildren but wish to rent for a year or so until they feel they have some knowledge of the local market.

My friend Barry and his brother enjoy working with this tenant group and now deliberately promote their 'street houses' or terraced properties towards these retired people saying 'they are careful to always pay their rent on time, even bringing it into the office weekly. They take good care of the houses and treat them as if they were their own.'

It's your move

How you begin your first move into having rental property and then into developing a portfolio of a few properties is very much your call. Look at the opportunities and research the best fit of property and tenant type to your own character and expectations. Just as with other investment decisions, it is probably wise not to have all your money in one set type of property and a balanced portfolio is likely to contain some variety of both buildings and tenant groups.

LANDLORDS TALKING – PETE

Based in the Midlands, but with a shop-fitting business that has seen him work across the UK, Pete has bought a block of rental property that contains 12 bedsits, six flats and a ground floor shop. He used a 40 per cent deposit that he had built up over time.

'The property is in an area not highly regarded locally, but I could see that with a bit of a clean up externally and a refurbishment of the individual units, there was scope for a good cash flow and I could attract professional working tenants.'

'I was getting a bit tired of the driving and the aggro involved in shop-fitting work and wanted to gain the revenue while staying closer to home. The block was £280 000 and brings in rents of just under £50 000. It has taken me a few months to get it looking good again and in that time I haven't had any tenants upstairs, but the property is already worth a lot more now I have refurbished it.'

Pete finds the tenants through advertising locally and arranges the payment of rent directly to his account. If tenants have a problem he expects them to call him and living close makes this easy.

'I'll wait until this is running well and next year I think I'll get a similar block of flats and repeat the process. The second time round I hope I'll make fewer mistakes.'

Choosing the right area and property

In theory you can attract tenants for any property anywhere – provided the rent is low enough. But this approach will never make you any money! You must buy property in areas where your tenants will want to live.

Who makes a good tenant? People who are in changing careers, full-time education, at the start of their careers or are new to urban centres will always be on the lookout for good quality, well-priced accommodation offering value for their money. You are looking for students wanting to live close to the college campus, recent graduates just starting their careers, medical staff close to hospitals, divorcees wanting to live close to their children, people without work in the former industrialised towns and cities. With students and medical staff it is easy to locate property geographically.

In your home town

The advantages of buying property locally are many. You know the area well, and may be able to hear of property coming up for sale before it goes to the estate agents. Because of local knowledge you have a 'gut feel' or sixth sense about whether a house in such and such an area will attract which sort of tenants.

Perhaps you can tell which side of the estate or which side of the road is easiest for getting into work or shopping areas using public transport. You don't have to take the word of the estate agent on everything, and I think this gives you more strength sometimes in making your offering to buy. The chances are strong that you can put together a small team of builders, decorators, and repairers to look after the property or portfolio of properties you end up having.

The final benefit of having property nearby is that you can be on hand quicker, and for many landlords this is important. If you are collecting money yourself there are clear benefits. If you are using the services of a letting agent, the location does not matter and you can choose more broadly.

Away from your home town

We have never owned property close to home. For me to get to see our tenants in London has always involved a three-hour drive. Yet the benefits have been considerable. If you have a house in an area which commands good rent and live yourself in an area where either mortgages or rent are low by comparison, then it is possible for you to benefit strongly by receiving a rental income, even on one property, that is greater than your own accommodation cost.

I did that comfortably for more than five years. One small property in an unfashionable part of London grossed more rent than our rent to a landlord in rural Nottinghamshire. Might this be something for you to explore? Could your lifestyle benefit from a rental income that covered your own biggest bill each month? With the use of telephones and e-mail, particularly if you are self-employed, or work in creative or people-focused businesses, there is far more opportunity than ever before for you to work from home for part of the week and go to see work colleagues and clients on the other days.

Look at this location topic from a different angle. As a rule of thumb, the further away you are from London the lower the price of properties. The further you are from an area of a town which is fashionable or desirable, the less you are likely to pay for a property. However, the closer you are to good train networks between cities, or to decent bus and train networks in and around cities, the more attractive your property becomes, no matter how unfashionable the area.

The real value in understanding this process is that you can use your money to buy property in towns where property could cost around half of what it might cost to buy in your own area. For the sake of an illustration I have looked at house prices in undervalued areas of towns along the M6 and M1 motorways. None of the houses is in the best area, they are simply reflecting what you can find with careful searching. Neither have they been selected as areas of premium rental income. These are properties where you can get the same rent month after month and find tenants who are likely to stay at least a couple of years or where your empty periods of letting are reduced to the minimum.

Figure 12.1 gives examples taken from towns to show the differences in prices you might expect to pay between one town and the next. I have

Figure 12.1 Real examples of two-bed terraced houses suitable for renting (including repossessions)

Liverpool	£15 000	–	£20 000
Stoke-on-Trent	£15 000	–	£25 000
Leeds	£25 000	–	£30 000
Whitby	£45 000	–	£55 000
Newark	£40 000	–	£45 000
Nottingham	£45 000	–	£55 000
Leicester	£40 000	–	£50 000
Daventry	£50 000	–	£80 000
Northampton	£60 000	–	£80 000
Milton Keynes	£80 000	–	£100 000
Luton	£75 000	–	£120 000
Outskirts of London	£100 000	–	£150 000

tried to show in this listing from north to south how your money can often buy more in the north.

Simple assumptions

No matter what the location, there are some factors that can be assumed.

■ Three bedrooms are easier to let than two-bedroom properties and represent better value for your money.

■ The tenant also gets better value when they take on a three-bed property than a two-bedroom property.

■ Terraced houses all over Britain are similar in build construction and if they have been strong for 100 years or more, they will very likely be strong for many years to come.

■ They are a standard type of house that tenants, landlords and letting agents all know and understand well. This is also true for the builders, electricians, and decorators you may be using.

■ It takes only half an hour on the phone to track down the estate agents in half a dozen locations you do not know well and to get on their mailing lists. From the material they send out, you will get a feel for those you can rely on. In turn, the good agents will be able to put you in touch with their preferred letting agents. You can use the same approach to get a weekly subscription to a local newspaper on the night their property pages come out.

Figure 12.2 Better returns away from London

Town	Purchase	Monthly rent	Annual income	Gross margin
Liverpool	£10 000	£200	£2 400	24%
Stoke-on-Trent	£15 000	£240	£2 880	19%
Leeds	£25 000	£300	£3 600	14%
Whitby	£25 000	£300	£3 600	14%
Newark	£30 000	£600	£7 200	16%
Nottingham	£35 000	£600	£7 200	20%
Leicester	£40 000	£500	£6 000	15%
Daventry	£45 000	£600	£7 200	16%
Northampton	£50 000	£600	£7 200	14%
Milton Keynes	£80 000	£750	£9 000	11%
Luton	£75 000	£800	£9 600	13%
Outer London	£100 000	£900	£10 800	11%

Generally speaking this means you will keep more money in your pocket when you buy a property in an area where that property costs you less to buy. Figure 12.2 demonstrates this and is focussed on repossessed or distressed property only, bought at the usual discounts below standard values. I hope these rough figures speak for themselves and show you just what you can achieve for your money. On the examples shown, 15 per cent return on your money is not that difficult to achieve and you simply need to do some shopping around. Where else other than property could you make a 15 per cent gross return and still control the asset that generated the income in the first place?

There is probably no finer form of testing and research than spending time looking at the return on investment you want to achieve and working through the numbers. I hope this exercise has revealed to you the real value of being prepared to at least consider investing outside of an area that you know.

Finding the right property

In looking for the right property, avoid the common mistake of purchasing a house or flat because you like the look of it or think it is cute! Instead put your money into one which will appeal strongly to tenants.

Buy the local newspapers and gazettes on the day they advertise local property. If you don't live in the area ask them to send you this each week. Then telephone all the agents and ask them to recommend the areas which rent the best and the most consistently. Get on their mailing list as a potential investor, and ask for their landlord's pack. This will include details of property they have for rent and property suitable for a rental investment. This way you can do your homework from one mailing.

Tell the estate agents you work to strict pricing/bedroom criteria and hold your ground. Most agents will always send you properties at the top-end of your budget because they make more commission this way. Find an agent you can trust to bring you good deals. Watch out for them trying to promote one-bed studio flats and maisonettes. This is fine if you are looking at a city with a very fluid population and you are buying in the central district because you want to rent to urban dwelling city workers seeking tiny properties. Elsewhere, think carefully about this type of unit and the difficulties that come with it.

At the other end of the scale, don't be tempted into buying one enormous house or a flat with four bedrooms because in most circumstances they will be slow to let and even slower to relet. Instead consider investing in three two-bed flats or two-bed terraced properties.

Using your criteria for return on investment, select a half-dozen properties and tour round them with your agent. Don't be afraid to take photographs or video, or to use a dictating machine to record your impressions of each property. Make notes about the street it is in as well as about neighbouring properties.

Never visit any property outside of full daylight. This is safer for you but it also means you see things as they are. You have every right to take a friend or adviser with you on these tours. They will see things you never notice. This could save you a lot of time and money. Always have either a camera or a video camera with you when you go to see properties. By the time you are ten minutes away from the house you have just seen, you will have forgotten half the features.

Figure 12.3 can be a useful aide-memoire to have with you when going to look at potential investments.

> Don't be afraid to take photographs or video, or to use a dictating machine to record your impressions of each property.

There goes the Neighbourhood!

You think you have chosen the right property in the right area for you to fill it with prospective tenants. Use Fig. 12.4 and the summaries below as a score card of the pros and cons of you successfully renting your property.

Figure 12.3

Property Viewing Record

Estate agent / Auctioneer ....
Address of the property ....
Type of property ....
Asking price ....
Date of first viewing ....
Date of second visit ....

Comments about the surrounding area
Schools   Traffic noise   Shops   Public transport   Business units

Outside
Garden and driveway
Garage
Window frames and glass
Walls
Drains and guttering
Roof

Neighbouring properties

Inside
Hallway
Lounge
Dining room
Kitchen
Utility room
Bedroom 1 (sizes)
Bedroom 2
Bedroom 3
Bedroom 4
Bathroom
Loft

Potential work required
Heating and plumbing
Electrical repair
Decoration
Damp patches
External lighting

General observations and things to remember
....
....
....

Figure 12.4 Locations and tenant types

Property location	Tenant type	Facilities	Rental opportunities
City-centre district	Single professional Busy lifestyle	Smart, well laid out Functional design Good furnishings Small kitchen	Premium rent Good capital growth
College towns	Groups of friends Students	Safe, big kitchen Big lounge Outside bike storage	Long-term rent over 2 or 3 years with summer void period
Small town	Divorced singles Couples in first home Company lets	Small garden Parking	Steady cash flow
Suburban and rural	People changing jobs New to the area Company lets	Garden Parking	Steady cash flow Slow capital growth

University   If the campus is within a mile or two from your flat then you will probably score well here. There will be a strong demand for property that is well-maintained, clean, dry and has a good landlord – you! Keep in with the student accommodation office and you could have a steady stream of revenue.

On the other hand, what happens during the ten weeks of summer holiday? Do you spend two weeks decorating it every summer and eight weeks wishing you had full-time tenants, or do you offer the students a slight reduction in rental over the summer period so as to ensure your house is always occupied? Think it through but the location overall could mean you are onto a winner.

Motorway junction   Provided it is within ten or 15 minutes' drive this can have a great beneficial impact on your house or flat. Many busy, working people want to be able to get on the road quickly each day for their jobs and this accessibility means you can be assured of a quick turna-round time between tenancies. Generally a plus point and a good move.

Two minutes drive from the same junction and you should be worrying. If a tenant is renting in a place where they feel the local environment is either noisy, smelly or dangerous they will not stay in the property for long. By inspecting a property at different times of the day you can become aware of the impact of the rush hour on local traffic, whether people are using the street as a 'rat run'. If your tenant market is busy professional people then buy property where they can have quick access to the road networks without living on top of them!

Fashionable address   Watch out for this one. The more you have to pay for a property the more nervous you get watching the gap between tenancies and the smaller the return on your investment generally. You can get tenants to fill these properties but they have to find the money and corporate lets are only feasible in certain postcode areas. For most of the country this is not relevant.

If you want to experience the benefit of capital appreciation but are a little short of the readies to begin with, buy in an adjacent area where the tenants are still close to these fashionable and trendy postcodes but without you having to pay stupid prices. If you can get a rent of £1000 on an ex-council flat close to a city centre and still retain a healthy profit, why would you want to pay through the nose for only a marginally better rent and use up much of your own investment funds on a heavy deposit? Remember your strategy and stick to it!

Public transport   This is a big one! If your tenants can be on a bus or a train within ten minutes' walk they will be keen to take the property on. Five minutes is even better. In the London market anything within five to ten minutes walk from a Tube station will command a better premium. The same is true of any of the bigger cities with their tram link services across the central routes.

If there are few transport links then ask yourself seriously who you are trying to attract as a tenant. If they do not use transport will they have their own car? Are they working and able to commute to earn money to pay your rent? Will they be so far removed in your property from friends and workmates that after three months they become lonely and move out? Be careful on this one.

Ex-council property   Where for many private buyers this does not appeal as a place to make their homes, these are often a landlord's dream. They are normally built to a good standard and you can buy a lot of bedroom for your pound. Semi-detached and terraced properties are plentiful and rent well to people who want to live and work in an area where they perhaps grew up, or where they can stay close to friends and family. In urban areas, ex-council high rise blocks provide the best views around. Your working tenants will get as much space on the city skyline as in many expensive warehouse and industrial building conversions that have cost three or four times as much. Unemployed tenants on the same estate may provide you with an income that – although slow to get started with the benefit office – can be as reliable or more reliable than the income from a working tenant.

On the downside, you may have one of just a few privately purchased properties within a large and run-down estate. Avoid these. Instead look to buy flats or maisonettes on the outer edges of such big estates, close to public transport, schools and shopping facilities.

Schools and catchment areas   Where a school has been judged to be of a high standard, parents will move as close as possible to be able to get their child into the school without having to pay for private education. This demand can be very strong and push house prices up significantly close to the school. This means that if you can rent out a property close to such a school you can expect demand to be high from professional people, perhaps on a corporate let. The implication is that you can stand to receive good capital appreciation on your original investment while the tenants cover the mortgage until you want to sell.

However, pricing around good schools can be prohibitive to the flow of investing landlords, given that they know what margins they want and can see what the rental sector will stand.

Shopping and local leisure   Big-brand, fast-food restaurants, out-of-town shopping centres and good designer pubs within a few miles of your property will again make the rental easier. Where the amenities are of good quality there will be good demand from tenants who want to be able to shop, dine and socialise within a short distance of their new home in your flat or house.

Where there is a lack of such facilities or where shopping is unsafe and streets are awkward after dusk, you will find the rentals equally unattractive. Take care to think about why a property is so cheap in the agent's window. Why is it such an apparent bargain at auction? Fig. 12.5 provides a warning.

Parking   With cars so cheap and finance so easy to come by, most of your tenants will be drivers with at least one car. If you are letting to a

Figure 12.5

Why so cheap?

I recently looked at some good terraced housing in a major city in central England. I went round three properties one afternoon with the agent and liked them all. Each one was selling for under £10 000 where the normal price for a good terrace was around £25 000.

Ever keen to make an investment, I asked a local builder to meet me at the houses later the next day to assess the cost of decoration and any renovation work.

After dusk I realised why they were so cheap. Within a stone's throw there were two 'massage parlours' and on the same road for a quarter of a mile in both directions there were several 'working girls' standing below lamp posts or in the shadow of trees. So much for the good investment. Do your homework first!

couple or to a group of friends who share the tenancy, there may be two or three cars that need to park nearby. This is fine if you have a large driveway to the property or if there is plenty of land around the house. But this may not be the case. Get properties where parking outside is straightforward, either on a driveway or at the roadside.

> Where parking is difficult, where roads are narrow and driving is cramped, things can work against the rental of the property.

Where parking is difficult, where roads are narrow and driving is cramped, things can work against the rental of the property. People are territorial animals and like to park their cars within a hundred yards of their house, if not right outside. Narrow streets and few parking bays simply cause aggravation. No one wants to go to their car in the morning and find a wing mirror smashed or a body panel scratched.

Hospitals Just like having a university near to your investment, a hospital on your doorstep can be a great source of tenants and the effective route to consistent rental cash flow. Hospitals have their own accommodation teams to help staff find a place to sleep, so make friends with such people and keep your properties in good condition.

The fastest way to be thrown off the list of a hospital accommodation office is to misrepresent your property or not to maintain it once you have hospital staff renting from you. No one likes a bad landlord and the message spreads fast.

Flooding The memory of recent downpours and the sight of Britain underwater has forced the introduction of flood risk insurance premiums. In such areas you will not get insurance for properties and in certain postcodes you are even less likely to get a mortgage at the terms you want one. Check that your intended property is not in a flood zone and if in doubt err on the side of caution and avoid the purchase altogether.

LANDLORDS TALKING – ALEX

Alex rents out three properties in west London. One is in a 1930s purpose-built block, one a basement in a converted Victorian terrace and the third is an 1880s maisonette. They have been bought over a five-year period; all with buy-to-let mortgages.

'I initially rented out my first flat when I went travelling three years ago and realised it was easy money. I then bought the other two with a conscious intention to rent them out as a long-term investment. No great strategy, but I do always read about property in the papers and research the areas I have bought in. I am financially very organised and very aware of what I can afford and how much things cost. This has probably made me more cautious than other investors, but has given me greater peace of mind. I work at being a good landlord and will replace or fix things properly, rather than let them slide. As yet, none of my tenants has moved out.'

She found the tenants via either an estate agent or a letting agency service. She manages the properties herself, speaking with the tenants regularly.

'With these three and a fourth one that I am looking for in Brighton, I have a full portfolio in my opinion and am living the life I love.'

On getting started Alex makes a comment echoed elsewhere. 'I wish I had had the confidence to start earlier. My regret is that I did not buy two or three flats at the same time in London before prices went mad.'

Managing the property

A great deal is expected of you when you become a landlord and it is worth reviewing the responsibility you have for the well-being of the tenant or tenants.

The legal framework

The first definition of your relationship as a landlord to your tenants comes from the use of legal structures and particularly the use of specific tenancy types. There are three main types of tenancy and it is worth you understanding these from the start.

■ *The assured tenancy.* Virtually all tenancies given nowadays are of this type. Under this format, the tenant has the right to exclusive use of all or a part of a property, and the landlord has the right to charge a market rent for the tenant's use of the property. The 1988 Housing Act gives the landlord the right to take repossession of the property where the tenant is in rent arrears of more than two months.

■ *The assured shorthold tenancy.* This shorthold tenancy is a sub-set of the assured tenancy. It gives you as landlord the right to recover the property at the end of the fixed term. This means that on a six-month assured shorthold tenancy you can have the property back at the end of month six. This form of tenancy is the most commonly granted tenancy.

■ *The Rent Act tenancy.* This is a tenancy granted before 15 January 1989 and is regulated by the Rent Act of 1977. Under this arrangement a landlord can charge only a 'fair' rent, whatever that is. Also, it is more difficult for the landlord to evict the tenant.

Where you go to an auction and read in the particulars of a property for sale, that the property includes a protected tenancy, it is very likely that you will have a tenant in that property who has been there since before January 1989. Because such tenancies are looked down upon as a potential source of nuisance or tenant difficulty, many will steer clear of them at auction. However, many landlords recognise the downward pricing effect that such a Rent Act tenancy can have on the sale price. They know that property is often undervalued as a result, and they will bid strongly for such properties. Their confidence is usually reflected in the much higher price of neighbouring properties.

If you want to buy properties that already have an existing tenant you must work with a solicitor who has skills in residential property conveyancing. Make sure you can find the date that the tenancy first started. Also, procure a copy of the original tenancy agreement as well as the most current version you can find.

Beyond the three tenancies described so far, there are also *licences* applied to the rental of property and these should be noted according to the activity you will be pursuing. When you rent a room in your home, the *lodger* has less rights than a tenant and can be evicted without resorting to a court order. The other area for licences to be used is with *holiday lets* where you can evict the occupiers if they refuse to leave.

Confusion is further caused over the classification of properties that can be either a licence or a tenancy. These can be 'houses in multiple occupation' (HMOs) where a number of people occupy the same property and are not a single 'household' unit.

Running a house in multiple occupation

According to the area you are buying property in, the definition of an HMO varies slightly. One council will have a different approach and definition to another. Given the volume of occupancies in an HMO it may be easier for the landlord to operate the premises than a letting agent. More occupants mean more potential troubles and so the greater the legislation a landlord has to comply with. The thinking behind this may appear flawed but essentially takes the view that if more can go wrong, it will. This leads to an expectation that such premises should have extra fire doors, smoke alarms, replacement ladders as escape routes and better facilities. You will need to keep all landings and passageways clear of clutter and obstructions, and ensure that kitchen facilities are maintained to a high standard. Living locally may work well in such circumstances, where you might expect more trouble from tenant groups.

Preparing the house

The following list covers the main points to consider.

- When preparing the house, notify your insurance company of any proposed tenancy and ensure the cover is adequate for current values.

- Make arrangements to have the gas, electricity and water meters read before each letting. Advise the local telephone company that a new letting is about to start.

- So you can be assured of the maximum potential rental, it is important that the house is thoroughly cleaned inside and out. Ideally the decoration of the house should be neutral throughout, so your property will appeal to the maximum number of potential tenants.

- It is your responsibility as landlord to ensure the building and contents are fully insured and you will need to produce evidence of this to any letting agent you choose to use.

- If the property is mortgaged already, you must get the written consent from your lender before letting. They are likely to agree to this if you show them that an economic rent can be achieved and that you will be putting the management of the property into the hands of a letting agent.

- If yours is a leasehold property, then in addition to seeking permission from the mortgagee, it is also important to check your lease to see whether you need the permission of the freeholder or the management company which represents them.

Health and safety requirements

When you rent out a property you undertake to ensure it is safe for people to live there. Bound up in this are several laws and acts with which you must comply. Failure to do so can be a criminal offence. If there is renovation work that needs to be done, make sure you carry this out before the tenants move in. To work around people can be both dangerous and expensive. If you attempt to botch things in an effort to save money, you will simply be wasting your time and money. Once a tenant discovers some work to be faulty, you could end up without a tenant and with an empty house. It is better to have the work done well and to a high standard than to have tenants who are only with you for a short time.

Also remember that if a tenant takes over a property that is well decorated, has obviously been kept clean and tidy, then at the end of the tenancy you have more chance of expecting your tenant to have maintained the property to a reasonable level. A case of what goes around, comes around.

Under the rules of the Landlord and Tenant Act 1985, you will be responsible for:

- heating and hot water fittings and appliances;
- structure and outside of the property;
- installations required for the installation of gas, electricity and water;
- compliance with the regulations outlined below will mean the safety of your tenants is protected and your reputation as a safety conscious landlord is guaranteed.

Furniture and furnishings

The Furniture and Furnishings (Fire) (Safety) Regulations 1988 (as amended in 1989 and 1993) are important if you expect to be a landlord. They require that the cover fabric and filling material of all the upholstered furniture in the property is made of fire-resistant material and able to pass what is known as the 'smouldering test' and 'match flame' resistant test and carry a permanent label confirming this.

Items that must comply with the regulations include all soft furnishings, upholstered furnishings, bed bases, mattresses, headboards, pillows, cushions and permanent or loose covers. Antique furniture is exempt as is other furniture made before 1950. Your failure to comply with these responsibilities is severe, resulting in a fine and or imprisonment.

Electricity

As the landlord you have a duty to ensure that any electrical items supplied as part of the letting process are safe. This includes the mains electricity supply. To keep abreast of this requirement, regular checks and tests should be made with up-to-date records maintained of the serial number and brand of the items, their condition and date of testing. If any equipment ever appears to be faulty or potentially unsafe you must remove it from the house immediately and replace it.

A further aspect of this is the Electrical Equipment (Safety) Regulations 1994. These require that any electrical items you supply as a landlord to your tenants are safe and have been tested by a qualified electrician. The regulations are enforced by the Trading Standards Office for the protection of both landlord and tenant. The items affected by the regulations include all 'portable appliances' as well as fixed items such as cookers and immersion heaters. Your failure to comply with these regulations may result in a hefty fine or a prison sentence.

Mark Bryant of the safety and renovation business Total Trade Services puts it this way... 'When you buy a property for renting out, it is your responsibility as landlord to ensure your tenants are safe throughout the day and when they go to sleep at night. Make every effort to have the same or greater level of safety checks for your tenants as you would for your own family. Fitters and installers of gas and electric equipment or supply are trained to the industry standards.'

This is a point well taken. Look at a potential investment property and ask yourself: 'Can I make this property up to a standard that would allow my family to live here and sleep peacefully at night, and still make a profit from the rental?' If the answer is yes, you can at least go to the next stage of considering the investment.

Gas supply

Under the Gas Safety (Installation and Use) Regulations 1998, a landlord must make sure that all gas appliances and equipment is checked by a qualified CORGI registered engineer before a new tenancy and annually after this first check has been carried out. A landlord's gas safety record will be issued once the engineer is satisfied that the installation meets current legislation. A copy of this must be given to the tenants before they start their tenancy.

> Landlords have been imprisoned for failure to comply with this regulation and where a tenant has died from gas poisoning.

Landlords have been imprisoned for failure to comply with this regulation and where a tenant has died from gas poisoning. To have annual servicing of your gas equipment and appliances is not enough to satisfy the legislation. It is vital you have a landlord's gas safety record. No letting agent will consider processing a new tenancy if you cannot furnish them with the record.

Carbon monoxide and smoke detection

Carbon monoxide gas is produced by all appliances that use fuel and these have to be checked regularly for safety and functionality. While there is no law requiring you to do it, a responsible landlord will probably want to provide carbon monoxide detectors at the property as an extra safeguard for the tenants. You can buy these from DIY stores.

In all homes built since 1992 it is requirement of building regulations that they are fitted with mains-operated smoke detectors. These should be installed on each floor and be interlinked. As a landlord wanting to protect the safety of your tenants you should install a smoke detector on each floor, usually on the hallway and landing areas. Again, these are easy to buy and simple to install.

Showing the property

When you have taken possession of the property and the frantic work of having builders, painters, plumbers, electricians, meter readers, letting agents and even your mum and dad work their way around the house is nearly done, it is time to get the new tenants to come and look around.

This begins as soon in the period of ownership as possible. Ideally you want to have prospects looking at the property right after you have given the building its first deep clean since you bought it. This may be before the workers have done their job and, if you are the workforce, before you have made any progress.

Allow a fortnight from the time of showing the property to having it occupied by a tenant. In the first week the letting agent will show people around, and hopefully from these prospects you will get a tenant. Clearly the success of these showings depends on the quality of the property, local demand and the time of the year. In small communities and even large provincial towns, the time of year can slow things down. I once waited a month to put tenants in a terraced house, but this was because we had bought it before Christmas. The same amount of space in London would have been guaranteed to have been taken by someone from the first people looking round in the course of an evening.

In the second week, the letting agent can do their work chasing references, recording your safety certificate on the property and ensuring the tenants have the resources to pay the rent each month.

When the property is ready for showing there are a few tips that will make it easier to rent:

■ Make the place as neat and tidy as possible. Get rid of the clutter. If there are still bags of rubbish lying around, put them in your car rather than leave them inside the property.

■ Start up some plug-in air fresheners the day before. Air the rooms well without making the place cold.

- Perform magic with mirrors and lights. People want to feel they are getting something spacious and you can support this with a couple of large mirrors in the right places. Have some attractive lamps around the property to give off some warmth and create a softer atmosphere.

- If you have decorating and renovation work going on and the site is clean, the tenants will feel good about the work being done. Where you have repainted a house to make it 'rental ready', stick with light and neutral colours.

- Allow the viewers to walk round the property on their own during their visit, perhaps for their second look after you have walked them round the rooms yourself. (When I view a property with a view to buying it, I always take a camera with me so I can remember it after-wards. If a potential tenant wants to do the same I have no objection.)

- If the letting agent is doing the viewings make it your responsibility to dress the rooms. This can mean putting colourful and attractive hand towels and some bath oils in the bathroom. Perhaps put some flowers in the living room, or a couple of small pictures on a bedroom wall. Just enough to give the place a homely feel to it, and not enough to make it seem like an overwhelming style.

Such efforts can mean the difference between you getting your rent within a fortnight of taking on the property, or making your first mortgage payment without a sniff of a potential tenant. Figure 13.1 gives a last-minute checklist of the main points.

Working with a letting agent

The first time you get involved in renting out a property it is safest for you to use the services of an experienced letting agent. The service they offer has three main aspects:

- to obtain the best rent;
- to select the right tenant;
- to ensure the tenancy agreement is properly prepared in accordance with the Housing Act of 1988 and which guarantees the landlord possession of the property at the end of the tenancy.

A *letting service* should provide the following:

- An initial inspection and rental evaluation from a qualified chartered valuation surveyor.

Figure 13.1 Landlord's last-minute checklist

Appliances Have you put all the instruction manuals and leaflets in the property so the tenants can work the machinery and know who to call with technical or service guarantee questions?

Cleaning Before the tenants move in, ensure the place has been professionally cleaned. Interpret this as you want, but the property must be seen to be immaculate on the day they move in. If you do pay people to clean the property you can claim this as an expense.

Consents and permissions The consent of a freeholder or a lender may be required for you to rent out the property. Failure to obtain such consent may make your mortgage or insurance invalid.

Insurance It is your responsibility to insure the building and the inventory contents. Where your ownership is leasehold only, the freeholder is liable for the buildings insurance, but you should always check this.

Inventory To save a lot of time and trouble at the end of a tenancy, have a professional inventory clerk produce an inventory. They will work through this with the tenant at the start of the tenancy and check things in again at the end of the tenancy before any deposit is repaid.

Keys Provide at least three sets to the tenants and a couple of sets for the letting agent. Keep your own set, but don't use them. From now on you need permission to go back into your house!

Post If you lived in the property before renting it out, arrange for your mail to be redirected to your new address.

Rules and regulations Does the property and the appliances and equipment in it comply with relevant regulations? Make sure they do.

Telephone bill Speak with BT or your local cable provider to have the account taken over by the tenant. You can get the letting agent to do this, but there is no harm in ringing to ensure your name has been removed from the billing details.

Utility bills and accounts Make sure these are transferred to the tenant's name from the start of the tenancy and that you or the letting agent makes a record of the meter readings on the day of handover. (If the electricity is on a card account, make this clear to the tenants so you don't get a call from them after a few days saying there is no electrical power in the property).

- Taking the details of the house and preparing the information for prospective tenants.
- Advertising the property in the local papers, on their website and circulating the details via their mailing list of people seeking somewhere to rent.
- Arranging to accompany people around the property.
- Interviewing potential tenants, obtaining references and negotiating the agreement between you as the landlord and the successful applicant.
- Preparing the tenancy agreement under the terms of the Housing Act of 1988 and protecting your position as landlord with regard to regaining possession of the property at the end of the tenancy.
- Agreeing the inventory with the tenant at the start of the tenancy.
- Ensuring the tenancy agreement is signed by the tenant and collecting one month's rent in advance together with a deposit equal to one month. They only release the deposit after a final inspection of the house.

The amount you would pay for this service to find a tenant would be around the equivalent of a week's gross rent.

A full *management service* is different and would give you the following benefits:

- The regular collection of rents.
- Accounting to you as landlord each month.
- Inspecting the property regularly to ensure everything is fine.
- Investigation of complaints.
- Getting the repairs done, by skilled people.
- Advising you when the contract is up for renewal.

A reasonable rate to pay for this might be 10 per cent of the monthly rental amount. Even if the fee was as high as 15 per cent consider what the cost would be to yourself of having to try and organise all this yourself.

Finding tenants

If you use a letting agent for a property then the process is relatively simple – they do the work and find the tenants. If you are doing the job yourself

> If you use a letting agent for a property then the process is relatively simple – they do the work and find the tenants.

you might take a more oblique approach to finding people. This will probably include you placing adverts in the classified section of newspapers and magazines, as well as cards in the windows of local newsagents and other shops close to the property. Tell everyone you know that you have a vacant flat or house becoming available and consider handing out a simple A4 sheet on the property and its facilities and location to those who express interest. Use the internet and get listings with the local accommodation office for students or within the local community website pages if for a broader base of tenant.

Checks and references

Ensure the references you collect from your tenant are produced on company stationery at their place of work. You can then find your tenant if you should need to and can make contact with them easily. In my experience people can only hide things from you when no-one around them knows they have skipped the rent or trashed a property. If there is any likelihood of others close to them getting to know this, then your house and belongings are far more likely to be treated respectfully and with care.

Once you have a reference, always make contact with the person acting as the referee. Play safe and ask for two references to give you slightly more leeway and a clearer understanding of your potential tenant. If one reference is an employer, consider asking for the second to be from a recent former landlord who you can contact and, in writing, ask the landlord about the rent having been paid on time and in full each month, what was the state of the house when they left and so on.

The advantage of this is that if the landlord is relatively local you can each learn from each other about where your properties are, how much you each charge, if you have no available property when someone enquires you can refer them to the other landlords you know. Do this on the basis that what goes around comes around and you could benefit too.

Pay a little extra to have a complete financial credit check on the potential tenants. A few pounds invested now could save you a huge amount risked later.

One further point about checks. Follow your intuition on whether a tenant will be right for you and your property. This is not a black and white rule based on logic, but your own gut feeling about someone will often be right. If you have doubts about a potential tenant, you will do best to leave well alone.

Working with students

If you want to be successful as a student landlord, invest the time in building strong relationships with the college or university accommodation office. This will always be a dedicated team who have the well-being and interest of students very high on their agenda. Such people are highly influential in having your name added to or removed from a list of landlords considered by the university or college.

Make contact with the accommodation office and ask for their landlord pack. This will outline demand for property in the area, explain ways that the student population needs to be served through the standard and type of facilities and detail schemes operated locally. For example, several university towns have an environmental audit of the property offered by the local council that can part-fund property improvements such as double glazing, cavity wall insulation, the installation of safety alarms and the fitting of motion-activated lights outside.

Good student landlords understand that in the student population – faster than any other tenant group – if you get things wrong or you become too greedy, you will lose your income virtually overnight.

If you have a connection with a university town because you have a son or daughter attending, consider buying a property there for a number of reasons. You will know largely where they are; you can guarantee receiving more rental income than the cost of purchase; that over the three or four years that your child is there, the property is likely to appreciate in value by more than the cost of the maintenance and overheads; once the property becomes vacant when your child leaves, it will already be well-known to other students.

Remember that the property will be empty for as many as ten weeks over the summer. This is a good time to catch up with maintenance and redecoration. Some students are happy to pay a retainer at a lesser rate than their normal weekly rent in order to stay in the house over the summer. Think hard about charging a retainer. It will often be better that you tell the tenants when the property will be redecorated and keep the house available to them.

Do not even think of investing in property in a student town unless you are prepared to play by all the rules.

Doing it yourself

Where you live close by it can be worth managing the property yourself without resorting to the use of a letting agent for anything except the initial finding of tenants and completion of the tenancy agreement. Considering the fact that you will typically pay 15 per cent for a full management service every month, it can seem attractive to deal directly with the tenants yourself. Many private landlords opt to do this, figuring that once they have the tenants in and the rent is being paid under a tenancy agreement they will have few major troubles, and certainly none that they could not handle.

There will inevitably be times when you wish this were not the case, such as the call that asks you to come and help them with the flooded washing machine or the lawnmower blade that needs sharpening. On these days you will probably learn something about your lazy tenants that you did not know before and at least it gives you the chance to look at the property again.

It is common for landlords who are managing properties themselves to go to the house or flat every three months and spend some time looking at the condition of the property and speaking with the tenants about whether they need anything.

Working with tenants

Your tenants have rights of their own when they rent from you. These include the right to live in a tenanted property as if it were their own home with the landlord having to give permission before entering the property. While you have a right to inspect your property or to carry out repairs, you must give the tenant 24 hours written notice and comply with the conditions in the original tenancy agreement. The visits you make must be at what are considered to be 'reasonable times of day' and not be restrictive for the tenant.

When you have a good tenant, and this does mean virtually all tenants, you can work with them to ensure the relationship is a good one. This might mean keeping in regular contact because you collect the rent money and see them weekly or monthly. It could mean calling to visit them and inspect the property every quarter, or it might involve visiting once or twice a year, but telephoning at other times to speak with the tenant.

What matters is that the tenant does not misunderstand the calls or visits as you being overly nosy or concerned about their tenancy, but that they realise your rights and empathise with your concerns.

Finding replacement tenants Something I have done for a number of years is make it clear to a tenant that I will be grateful for them finding a replacement tenant once they move on. This takes the form of a cash payment, equivalent to perhaps a week's rent, but saves me the trouble of starting from scratch. For the tenant who wants to help and gets involved with this process it can seem very easy. In the time they have enjoyed living in the property they will have had friends over, organised social events in the house and generally treated it as their own place for entertaining and socialising. In this time some friends are bound to have commented on the quality of the place or the ease of access it has to transport. The reasons could be many and varied, but allow the tenant to think of the people most likely to want to take on the property. You still need to do the checks and references, but you will be dealing with someone who wants the property and has known of it for some time.

Accepting housing benefit

While some will refuse to have anything to do with tenants receiving benefit, there are probably a greater number quite willing to have tenants receiving benefit included within their rental portfolio. Because of the initial delays in getting payments set up and instructions to pay directly to yourself, it may be sensible to avoid this tenant group on your first let. However, once you have three or four properties let to working people and have established a cash flow, consider a new move.

The plus point about receipt of housing benefit is that the money is paid as regular as clockwork provided there is no change in the circumstances of your tenant. In many areas of the country, unemployment conditions are still such that there are thousands of people on benefit. In such areas, there is little chance of re-employment and so these benefits are likely to continue for the foreseeable future. Where sickness is a factor, the security of protection against non-payment is further enhanced.

Any tenant receiving housing benefit from a local council will probably have a relative in full employment willing to guarantee any arrears during the tenancy. This will give you some peace of mind and can be a useful additional piece of security.

The monies paid for rental purposes can be paid directly to your account by the authorities and you should insist on this being the case before the tenant completes any tenancy agreement with your agent or yourself. Do remember that in the event that a tenant is shown to have been fraudulently claiming benefit, the authorities can currently look to you for the arrears going back as far as six years. You have been warned!

Houses in the neighbourhoods of highest unemployment tend also to be the cheapest properties and so the benefit monies will usually be sufficient to pay the going rent in such an area. The monies allocated for rental are always intended to cover the market rate so you as landlord receive the same rent as you would from a working tenant in the same property.

The deposit always has to be provided by the tenant or a family member such as the guarantor suggested earlier. The benefits office will not cover the deposit. The fact that the tenant has to find the deposit is also a plus point for you since they are emotionally attached to the deposit at least.

Deposits

Deposits are a thorny topic and one to get most landlords into a heated discussion. The deposit when taken by a letting agent will be placed into a separate client account and lodged in a building society or bank for the period of the tenancy. I have never known the deposit to be returned by any agency complete with the payment of the interest earned, although this topic is raised every few years in the media. By contrast, there are many landlords who will open a simple account marked in the client's name and will pay interest back to the tenant.

The deposit is typically a month or six weeks' worth of rent and is accepted on the basis of being a surety for good treatment of the property and its contents. For you to hold back the deposit for the wrong reasons can land you in a lot of trouble and this is an issue that aggrieved tenants will fight tooth and nail for long after they have left the property if they consider they have a case.

Normal wear and tear is something you cannot deduct from the deposit; you should be claiming this with your accountant as a legitimate expense. Accidental damage to the property is something you should claim from insurance where appropriate. By all means deduct money for wilful damage or total neglect of the furniture, but claiming too much for the wrong reasons will only make you an enemy of the tenant or gain a poor reputation for landlords in general because of your stance.

A couple of years ago some tenants left taking with them crockery and cutlery, a set of dining chairs, a coffee table and every cooking implement in the property. They had also damaged a sofa and two armchairs by cigarette burns. One window had been cracked and not reported, and two armchairs had been left in the garden, obviously through several seasons of weather! The costs of the replacements would have been more than twice the deposit, but the items had been in the house for several years before that two-year tenancy had started. I simply chose not to return the deposit and listed the reasons and the costs in a letter to the tenants at their forwarding address. They made no further claim.

The other protection you can create with younger tenants is to ask for a written guarantee from their parents that in the event of an unresolved dispute with yourself, the parent will stand as guarantor for non-payment of rent or damage to the property. This really has no value on its own but means that the tenants are more likely to take their responsibilities seriously and look after your property in the first place.

What about when it goes wrong?

Perhaps a tenant has stayed on when they were supposed to move out at the end of their tenancy. In such circumstances how do you go about regaining control of the situation and of your property? Whatever your feelings about the situation, do not try and evict the tenant yourself. Leave your big and strong friends out of the loop and don't even think about changing the locks or nailing up the front door. Any of these activities can land you in far more trouble than you can imagine.

You will have heard the same stories as me, namely that landlords do things like throw a tenant's possessions out onto the street when the rent has not been paid, or perhaps they harass them until they move out freely. Such stories are true but the landlords who do these things risk being taken to court by their tenants and being beaten by the law.

Behave yourself, keep your nerve and the property should be yours again swiftly.

The contract you issued at the start of the tenancy gives you much of the protection through 'mandatory grounds for repossession' of the property. This is a quick process and gives you the property again within just three to six weeks under what is loosely termed the 'accelerated possession' process. Under this system you will be claiming possession on the grounds that:

- You are in arrears with a mortgage arranged before the rental activity commenced and the lender wants the property to sell and realise their loan.

- The tenant is a least two months in arrears on their payments to you or a letting agent acting for you.

- You are seeking to redevelop the property and need to have the tenant out before you can start work.

- The property was your home previously and you wish to return to it.

Slightly different, are the grounds considered 'discretionary'. These allow for you to take back possession of the property where it can be clearly demonstrated that the tenant:

■ Was in arrears with the payments of rent at the time you started the court proceedings or served notice of repossession.

■ Is in breach of any other aspect or term of the tenancy agreement.

■ Acquired their tenancy under false pretences or through deception.

■ Has damaged the furniture in the property.

■ Has personally smashed up the property or allowed someone else to trash the place.

When the property is empty

Once the property is vacant again, it is time for you to take stock of the condition of the property and the garden. Do you need to repaint the whole house, or just a few rooms? Will it be better to replace the carpet on the ground floor with wood-effect flooring that will make it easier to rent and easier to look after if your tenants are busy working people? (By the way, if you accept pets in your property then a wood flooring on the ground floor will help greatly and mean you never have to haggle over a carpet damaged by a cat or dog.)

The day the tenants move out is the best day for you or the letting agent to visit the property and check on its condition. Photograph the property if you want to.

Do an inventory check between yourself and the tenant just before they move out, or ask your letting agent to do this. There is generally a flat fee for an inventory check and you should allow as much as £100 for the time taken by the professional clerk who will complete this task.

You will hopefully have given the letting agent notice that the property would be available for reletting from a certain date. Ask them to inspect it with you after the tenants have moved out. Seek their opinion on what should be done before the next rental and what facilities or items might be replaced or introduced. Then establish a schedule to make good any redecoration or damage and have new tenants in the property as soon as possible.

LANDLORDS TALKING – PHILIP

Philip is a plumber who employs a small team within his business. He has three rental properties in and around a small market town and bought the first five years ago. It was a two-bed flat in a historic mill conversion, bought for £40 000 and now valued at £60 000. It brings in £100 a week and is let to a working couple.

The second property is in a mill conversion in a different part of town. This was bought a year ago for £66 000 and brings in rent of £475 per month.

The third property is a two-bed terrace property bought in a poor state for £60 000. He is putting in a loft conversion for a third bedroom or office and expects to bring in £550 per month once finished. 'Doing the work myself should save me money and add £15 000 to the value,' he says.

'I collect the rent myself at the moment, but once I have a couple more I shall ask the local agent to manage them all for me. It can be a lot of hassle to collect the money myself and I am not sure whether it is worth it.'

The properties are mortgaged at between 75 and 95 per cent.

'I wanted to get a property just to give myself a bit of security from the day job. Now I have three built up over five years, and I can see myself getting this number again over the next two years. So far I have bought through estate agents, but I think I shall buy others at auction. I reckon that when I have eight I will be able to take some real benefit from them. Right now I have to work very hard to support my hobbies and my enjoyment of travelling. When my daughters are older I hope the houses will allow me to provide well for them financially.'

The UK holiday lettings market

A place in the country? Somewhere down by the seashore? A farmhouse in the hills or a cottage in a market town? The beauty of the holiday lettings market is that it gives you the chance to choose an investment in a place where you already feel at home. The holiday lettings market is an interesting one that can provide you with the attractive mix of good income and also buy you a property in a location that you enjoy for your own breaks.

How it works

Unlike the conventional rental market, where letting is usually for a six-month minimum period, the holiday market might only give you 20 weeks or so of revenue. However, the revenue you take on these lettings can be three or four times the conventional rate for each week that you have holidaymakers in your property. Hence your return can be as high as twice the normal income that might be expected.

In the holiday lettings market there are some important issues. These include the location and construction of the property, the standard of accommodation you provide, the expectation you have of income, the type of holidaymakers you are expecting to cater for and how close you are to the house.

Location

People take holidays almost anywhere in the country, but this does not mean you should be too casual about where you buy a holiday property. Consider where you enjoy taking holidays. Is this the sort of place that you think would prove popular with other people? Do you want a property in a place that you have always loved or would you prefer this investment to take you somewhere new and interesting that you have never been to before?

Popular locations would include anywhere there is a national park, or sites of great natural beauty. Coastal towns, fishing villages, provincial market towns that have great architecture or castles, ancient minsters and famous abbeys, all have their appeal as places where peoples go to get away from it all. In just the same way, many people are attracted to visiting older cities around the country. Take the example of York. It is an ancient city with a wealth of visitor attractions and gets tourists all year round. A small compact town house would rent well, whether old or modern.

A small flat in a suburb of London, provided primarily for the American and Japanese tourist market would do well provided the standard of accommodation was in line with what these visitors expect. Anywhere people take holidays you can invest in property and make a profit.

However, if you don't like York or London, don't invest there. If you would prefer to spend time in the Forest of Dean or the Scottish highlands, then you should really give serious thought to having a property there. You will put more effort into the promotion of the cottage if it is in a place you love.

> It is likely that there will be at least the equivalent of three to six months when the property will not be rented out.

It is likely that there will be at least the equivalent of three to six months when the property will not be rented out and so you should look at the likelihood that you can enjoy time there yourself. If possible, buy a property where there is a decent view from the living room and from the bedrooms. People have enough of living in small places themselves and want to feel closer to something special when they are on holiday. The 'special' can be location relative to the centre of the market town, or being 300 yards from the beach. Perhaps you can see the seashore and the cliffs from the breakfast room window, or look across the river from the front of the house. People will associate the view with their memories of a good holiday and a decent view always gets a mention in the promotional literature.

Construction type

What sort of property do you fancy? From cottage to lighthouse to beach villa to modern flat, there is so much scope for you to have a unique building for holiday rental. Shop around at auctions. Make contact with building societies and banks and see what instructions they may have to dispose of unwanted property. Just as repossessions are a good source of immediate profit in the conventional rental market, the same situation affects holiday properties. While a more unusual property may cost more, it can also demand a premium of as much as 10 per cent per rental over a standard cottage.

Standard of accommodation

Sylvia Stimson of Derbyshire Country Cottages says it beautifully when talking about what people expect from your cottage. 'Holidaymakers need to feel comfortable and safe in your holiday cottage so that they look forward to returning at the end of each day and are sorry to close the door for the last time at the end of their holiday.'

The most important element in creating this positive impression of your cottage is the quality of accommodation. This does not mean luxurious decor and overloading the property with accessories and kitchen equipment. Instead, we are referring to good quality furniture, a high standard of decoration and the use of fittings and fixtures which serve to complement each other and are in line with the style and atmosphere of the property.

Remember that penny pinching in this sector of the rental market will mean you never get repeat bookings and may well mean that the better letting companies will decline to deal with your property. Furnish it to the standard you would expect when you stay there yourself.

For your property to be accepted by a good professional holiday letting company the following summary explains what you must look to comply with.

Heating and services A safe, easily operated and well-maintained heating and water supply is essential throughout the property. Even in summer, people will want quick heating when the temperature drops. (Avoid the temptation to charge for the use of gas and electricity and instead provide an inclusive rental experience. People don't want the complication of meters, tokens and cards when they are on holiday).

Safety Furniture must comply with the Furniture and Furnishings (Fire Safety) Regulations 1988. Waste bins should be non-flammable. Have a powder fire extinguisher and a fire blanket in or close to the kitchen, and install smoke detectors around the property, usually on each landing and in hallways. Your local fire brigade will be pleased to supply literature about the siting of extinguishers and smoke alarms.

The lounge Sufficient seating in the form of sofas, armchairs, and an occasional table is essential. Also important is a good source of heat that is easy to operate. So while you may have a beautiful log fire or a wood-burning stove, also have radiators in the background. Good quality carpets or rugs are needed, as are a television and video player. If you have an open fire, provide coal and wood as well. Some landlords want to charge extra for this, others include it within the price. Feedback from the guests is always that they prefer to think of the fuel for the fire as free and seem to prefer this approach.

The kitchen   Enough space to move around sounds like a throwaway comment, but small kitchens result in complaints from holidaymakers who enjoy cooking in leisure. (Not so in the small city centre microflats where eating out is more common, but do consider this for rural properties away from eating establishments.) Provide a good work surface and hidden storage cupboards, together with a full-sized cooker (preferably gas), a microwave, fridge and a washing machine. If you have the space include a freezer, tumble dryer and a dishwasher. Ensure that the kitchen utensils and glassware are in good condition and that the crockery and cutlery sets are complete and of good quality. Whether the floor is timber, vinyl or tiled it should be free of hazards or snags that might cause a fall. It should also be easy to clean and you should make sure brushes, dust pans and mops are nearby.

The dining room   The seating should again be for the number of guests the cottage is advertised as accommodating. A table appropriate for the room together with a cupboard or sideboard for the storage of crockery and cutlery. Have a safe and clean high chair in the house for children.

The bathroom   A good suite of bath, basin and WC are essential. Increasingly holidaymakers are expecting showers. (American and Canadian visitors would expect to find a powered shower and might not book the property if one were absent). A bathroom cabinet, shelf and mirror. Space for the storage and heating bath towels and airing clothes. The larger the property the more need for a second WC and a second bath or shower room. As a rule of thumb, where you accommodate six or more people consider having two WCs and for eight or more people make sure you have at least two bath or shower rooms.

The bedrooms   Provide good quality beds and be prepared to replace these every few years to maintain the best accommodation. If it is a family property, have a child's cot and a sensible mix of double and single bedrooms. Have a full-length mirror in each main bedroom, and bedside tables and lamps by each bed.

Towels and linen At least one full set of linen should be provided. Towels should also be supplied on the grounds that people do not expect to have to find space for these in their luggage (on the way to the holiday I mean).

Leisure facilities If you have the space or the imagination and can provide a place for children to enjoy games and toys many guests will appreciate this. Also look to see if you can arrange or at least promote deals with the local swimming pool, health club, gymnasium or sauna.

Parking Since most people will get to the property by car it is important to provide parking for at least one car. Larger properties will usually have space for sufficient vehicles to accommodate the occupants of the house. If this is a challenge with your property, see if you can agree parking arrangements with your neighbours, the village hall, the local shop or public house.

Holidaymakers Will you be letting to walkers, climbers and ramblers? If so they can expect a different place than genteel folk on a quiet holiday. Different guests need their own tailored accommodation. For example, it would be a waste of your money to have a beautiful carpet throughout a house for people enjoying country pursuits if you did not also make sure they had the use of a boot room or enough space to take off their footwear. The same people would probably appreciate a downstairs shower and toilet just off the main entrance to the property.

> Will you be providing a romantic country love nest for couples or a place with several bedrooms for a family with children?

Will you be providing a romantic country love nest for couples or a place with several bedrooms for a family with children? How about space for the family pet? Maybe you draw the line at that request!

The key to successful letting of holiday property is deciding what role your cottage will play and what atmosphere you wish to provide for your guests.

What to provide in a holiday cottage

More so than ever your guests will expect a high standard of furnishings and equipment in the cottage, even to the point that the holiday property offers more luxury than their own home. Figure 14.1 gives a checklist that will help you to equip the property, room by room.

Figure 14.1   Equipment checklist

Lounge
- ☐ Sofas and armchairs
- ☐ Colour television and video player
- ☐ Supply of CDs
- ☐ Pictures, artwork
- ☐ Supply of coal and/or logs
- ☐ Visitor's book
- ☐ Occasional table/s
- ☐ Music system
- ☐ Box of toys, puzzles, board games
- ☐ Magazines, good quality paperbacks
- ☐ Fire starters and kindling
- ☐ Smoke detector

Kitchen equipment
- ☐ Gas cooker
- ☐ Fridge
- ☐ Washing machine
- ☐ Food processor
- ☐ Iron and ironing board
- ☐ Microwave oven
- ☐ Freezer
- ☐ Tumble dryer
- ☐ Coffee maker/percolator

Kitchen utensils
- ☐ Block of knives
- ☐ Carving knife and fork
- ☐ Wooden spoons
- ☐ Soup ladle
- ☐ Rolling pin
- ☐ Colander
- ☐ Scissors
- ☐ Cheese grater
- ☐ Corkscrew
- ☐ Bread knife
- ☐ Knife sharpener
- ☐ Spatula
- ☐ Sieve
- ☐ Serving spoons
- ☐ Potato peeler
- ☐ Tin opener
- ☐ Bottle opener

Kitchen crockery, cookware and glassware
- ☐ Milk jug and sugar bowl
- ☐ Soup and cereal bowls
- ☐ Cup and saucer set
- ☐ Egg cups
- ☐ Large meat dish
- ☐ Table mats
- ☐ Cheese board
- ☐ Sauce /gravy boat
- ☐ Roasting tins
- ☐ Various saucepans
- ☐ Beer glass per person
- ☐ Tumbler per person
- ☐ Plastic beakers for children
- ☐ Tea pot
- ☐ Set of large, dessert and side plates
- ☐ Mugs
- ☐ Large salad bowl
- ☐ Vegetable dish
- ☐ Condiments
- ☐ Bread board
- ☐ Milk jug
- ☐ Baking trays
- ☐ Small and large frying pans
- ☐ Wine glass per person
- ☐ Water jug

Figure 14.1 (continued)

Dining room
- ☐ Table with chairs for all occupants
- ☐ Sideboards and storage space
- ☐ Pictures and artwork
- ☐ Cutlery set
- ☐ Highchair for a child
- ☐ Shelving for accessories
- ☐ Indoor plants
- ☐ Lamps

Bathroom and toilets
- ☐ Cabinet and mirror
- ☐ Supply of matching towels
- ☐ Shower attachment if no shower
- ☐ Supply of toilet rolls
- ☐ WC brush
- ☐ Hooks for clothes and towels
- ☐ Glass or plastic tumbler
- ☐ Towel rack
- ☐ Non-slip bath and shower trays
- ☐ Bath and WC mats to be changed each let
- ☐ Toilet roll holder
- ☐ Waste bin and liners
- ☐ Shelf or window ledge space

Bedrooms
- ☐ Where possible, one double bed per room
- ☐ Pillow cases
- ☐ Bedside tables or cabinets and reading lamps
- ☐ Dressing table and small mirror
- ☐ Drawer space
- ☐ Duvets and covers
- ☐ Spare bed linen
- ☐ Child cot
- ☐ Pictures and artwork
- ☐ Two pillows per person
- ☐ Four spare pillows per property
- ☐ Alarm clocks
- ☐ Wardrobe or good clothes hanging space
- ☐ Set of clothes hangers
- ☐ Spare duvets and blankets for winter
- ☐ Mattress covers
- ☐ Spare sets of bed linen
- ☐ Smoke detectors on landing or corridor

Calculating the financial return

At a simple level this is done by multiplying the rental per booking by the number of bookings achieved. However, things are never quite so easy and it is worth looking at various aspects of the letting opportunity in more detail.

It can be tempting to jump into this market and gain the highest price per week with little or no forethought. In the short-term this may be attractive, but let's look at a profitable approach that will work for the longer term. Select a cottage letting agency that is charging sensible prices instead because your income will be maximised through securing a large number of confirmed bookings at decent rates rather than a few bookings at prices which are too much for many holidaymakers.

From the total income attained you will need to deduct the commission charged by the agent, the expenses of running the property and any taxes you may be liable for.

Guide to tax

Remember that you must seek professional advice given the complexity created by your own tax position and other earnings. Allowable costs include:

- The interest on a loan or mortgage taken out to buy the property or furniture and fittings within the property.
- Buildings and contents insurance, council tax or business rates.
- Professional fees such as accountancy costs, as well as agent's commissions and the charges for cleaning and caretaking.
- Maintenance and upkeep costs, including the redecoration of the property and the purchase of replacement furniture.

Remember that if your property is available for rentals for a limited period of the year you should only submit a bill for allowable costs for that pro-portion of the year in which you receive revenue. In this case, if your rental season were March to December inclusive and your family used the cottage in January and February, your claim of costs would be for ten months or ten-twelfths of the bills incurred.

Council tax or business rates

As the owner you are liable to pay either council tax or non-domestic rates (these are the business rates you pay on a holiday cottage).

Short season of rental   If your cottage is available to holidaymakers for letting for less than 140 days (this is 20 weeks) each year, then you simply pay the appropriate level of council tax on the property. Speak to your local authority about the category or 'banding' of the property to determine the charges.

Long rental season   With a period of availability that exceeds 140 days, the non-domestic business rate is applied to your property. In this case you should contact the local valuation officer to assess your property for business rates. At this point you will be liable to pay the business rate set nationally. This is paid as a fraction of a pound. For example, a property might be assessed as paying rates of £5000 a year at a rate of 50 pence in the pound. In this instance, you would pay £2500 and probably be asked to pay it over ten months at £250 per month.

Potential for change   January 2002 saw the presentation of draft documentation to government that may mark the beginning of the end of the traditional 50 per cent discount on council tax to second homeowners. If government can win the support for the abolishment of council tax discounts or for their severe reduction, then it is likely that the full rate of council tax will become payable on a rented cottage. This is unlikely to happen quickly, but it is important to be aware that it is likely to happen.

Value added tax

This tax is payable on anything deemed as a service, including holiday rentals. If your letting of your property is done as a small business with a separate identity from your other earnings and the turnover is less than the VAT registration limit, then there will be no liability for VAT.

   If this is the case, you will not have to charge VAT on the rentals paid by holidaymakers, but you will not be able to recover the VAT incurred in running the property.

   However, if you are letting the property as part of a business and you have elected to be registered for VAT, or are obliged by law to register because the rental turnover exceeds the limit, then VAT will be due on the rentals. If this is the case, VAT will be payable by you to Customs and Excise but at least you can now recover all the VAT you incur in running the property.

   For owners of one holiday property let for a long season, or perhaps two or three let for short seasons, it may be better to stay outside the VAT regime, but this can be a complicated matter and you would be well advised to seek professional advice on this.

Capital gains tax

Capital Gains Tax (CGT) will normally be charged on any financial gain you have made out of the sale of a cottage where it has increased in value since you bought it and where it is a property that has been used for some element of business use. The tax liability may be reduced if some of the following points are appropriate:

■ The property has been used at some time as your private residence.

■ You are over 50 years of age at the time of sale.

■ You reinvest the proceeds from the sale of the property in other business assets. This includes investment in other property for furnished holiday letting.

Selecting an area for a holiday property

When you look at the market for holiday lettings think long and hard about the way you wish to have access to the property, whether there are certain times of the year you are willing to let the property, and your reasons for making the investment.

Doing this allows you insight into the sort of letting agent you will want to work with. It is possible to select a national company to represent your property and be included in their brochure. This gives national exposure and ensures that tens of thousands of people look at the listing given to your building. However, you can look at it in a different way. Where do people want a holiday rental? By the seaside, in the mountains, or perhaps in the cities. Consider selecting an agent who knows a specific area and enthuses about it. In a time of niche marketing and specialist advice it may make a lot of sense to place your property in the hands of an agent who is such a specialist themselves.

To take the countryside example, consider a national park that you love. It could be the North York Moors, the Peak District or the Pembroke Coastline. Every year thousands of holidaymakers return to the same place they had a holiday last year or the year before. They will continue to visit an area they love. It is quite possible for you to have families who rent your cottage every year or every other year. They do it because they love the view, or the access to the beach, or the proximity to the footpath and the steam railway or the museum.

Will you want to buy within a small and tight-knit rural community where there is great pressure on local housing and difficulties for young people to buy their first property? Be careful here in that it is possible to buy a holiday rental property in such a community and cause offence and jealousy through your own limited use of the property in a beautiful area. If you are sensitive to the value of such a debate then perhaps consider instead buying a property where you feel you will make good use of it yourself on the occasions when it is not rented out to holidaymakers.

If this is the case, you have no advantage in advertising your property in a national directory of cottages, precisely because people so often return to the same location. You would do better to identify a company that just manages properties within a small area. This area may be a village or a cluster of villages and small communities. It may be that they manage property within a certain mountain range area, or along a certain coastline. Go and talk to these people. Ask their advice about the types of property that rent out well for holidays. The questions you should ask are the same questions you would ask of an estate agent in a more conventional working area but where people are still renting. Asking questions puts you in a position of control and is the fastest way for you to learn. Use questions to give yourself a quick insight into a community where you are considering an investment property.

What is the area like? Consider a list of likely questions. How far is the nearest cinema, restaurant, public house, church or café? What is the season for holiday lettings? Is there much demand for Christmas and New Year lets? What is traffic like in the summer? What sort of rents can I expect on a two-bed cottage as opposed to a four-bedroom barn conversion?

Sylvia Stimson recommends that 'you should ask the agent letting the cottage for a copy of their information pack for landlords. If they don't have a clue what to give you, then just walk out and go and talk to another agent. Generally speaking, if their literature for a landlord is of poor quality or seems unfocused, then you can make a safe bet that they are poor at promoting properties to potential holidaymakers.'

This is a good point and you don't need to get sucked into a poor investment or poor management of your property. You are buying a property with the express intent to make a return on your money. Remember this when you are looking at a 'chocolate-box cute' property that may not be the best investment, but which is easy to fall in love with. You are looking for a firm or an individual agent who has great knowledge of the area. Here are some pointers that are intended to help you in the search.

Selecting a letting agent

The right agent will work closely with you in a way that supports your own views on the rental of holiday properties. They will be looking to a long-term honest relationship with you as the property owner. Ideally they will provide a service that sees you recoup your investment and provides you with a steady stream of holiday rental income. Do your research thoroughly and ask lots of questions but here is a checklist to help you. The right agency will:

- Be patient with you as a new landlord to their books, even when you think you know what you are doing and yet clearly don't know the ropes!

- Be charging sensible prices that result in frequent and numerous bookings. You are better off with 25 weeks sold and paid for at £325 per week than holding out for £500 per week and having just a few weeks a year of income.

- Pay the deposit monies and rental fees to you as they are received. Some agencies, and it is usually the larger ones, keep hold of your money until after the holidaymakers have left and the let is deemed to be complete.

- Not have too many properties on its books. Better to be seen as a regional or a local specialist than to be attempting to be 'all things to all landlords'.

- Have a good booking conversion rate from enquiries. While the average conversion rate in the industry might be as low as 10 per cent per enquiry, you should be looking to work with an agency that can convert closer to 20 per cent of enquiries. Don't be afraid to ask them about how they maintain contact with first enquirers who have not booked anything.

- Will advertise throughout the year and not just the off season. This is crucial if you consider your property is a year-round proposition for rental. As a landlord, you want the maximum revenue from the property and it is worth finding a letting agency that works closely with you to fill every slot in the calendar you give to them.

- Provide with a good stream of rental income while not charging too high a commission. While 15 per cent is a standard charge for the managed rental of other residential property lettings, expect to be hit with higher charges for the rental of holiday property. Look at between 20 per cent and 30 per cent.

- Knows the local area inside out. Holidaymakers will have the most detailed questions about local activities, events, restaurants, museums and days out, and it will pay you dividends to work with a good local team.

- Be able to provide cleaning and caretaking staff for your property for welcoming guests upon their arrival, and for cleaning up between rentals. If you do not want to do this yourself, or if you live too far away, this service from your letting agent is worth its weight in gold.

- Have local representatives and staff on call to your guests. When someone is renting your cottage and something goes wrong, they will want to be seen within the hour. Ask your agency if they can guarantee this service and response time.

- Be able to let you see its marketing plan and initiatives for raising the profile of their cottage stock in front of potential holidaymakers.

LANDLORDS TALKING – ABOODI

Based in London, Aboodi has been a landlord since 1997. He had inherited money from his father's estate and wanted to put it to good use. He has several times bought property, rented it for two years and then sold it to realise the capital growth in cash. At the moment he has two properties up for sale, while already considering a further investment. He only uses mortgages for short-term finance and has already paid back the mortgage he had on an earlier property after just a couple of years.

'I use a professional letting agent to save me the time and hassle, even though I will sometimes find the tenants myself via an estate agent who knows me as a landlord.'

'Income is what I am looking for,' he says, and admits to never having worked with a specific strategy for his investment.

First time landlords should know 'that letting agents are worth it!' says Aboodi of the value he has received from professional help in starting and managing his rental income.

chapter fifteen

Overseas holiday lettings

With the introduction of the euro and the ease of cheap travel via budget airlines, it has never been easier to imagine owning a second property overseas. Just six hours driving time from Le Havre you can be unpacking at your property in central France. Within three hours flying time you could be anywhere in the Mediterranean and on several of the islands off the north African coast. A few more hours' flying takes you into the Caribbean and the Bahamas.

No matter where you select a second home for rental purposes it is essential to be aware of the process of buying overseas and how you will manage the rental of the property.

The scope for cultural confusion and misinterpretation of language means you must have the appropriate legal and fiscal awareness for the country or territory you are buying in. The rules and regulations in respect of the buying process, property title and tax position can be very different from systems in the UK.

With the Council of Mortgage Lenders telling us in 2002 that more than a million households in the UK own a second home, it is not surprising that lenders have been cautious about the way we sometimes buy these properties. Can the idyllic circumstances of a summer holiday mean that sense and reason leave us when we are away? Could it be true that many overseas properties are bought on the last day of the holiday just before we fly home to a grim dose of reality? Every year, thousands of properties in France, Spain, Italy and further afield are purchased with little rational behaviour being displayed!

Seduced by the holiday spirit and the fast talking patter of a sales person from a seashore development company, all too many people sign the dotted line and part with more than they bargained for. For you to consider an offshore investment, take the time to be thorough in your assessment and understanding of what life will be like there, whether you initially think you will be there for a few weeks or a few months of each year.

If you hanker after a farmhouse in Carcassonne or a chalet in the Alps, it is important to research the area, check your budget, and look out for the legal process in your target territory. If you fancy a villa in the Bahamas or a cottage on the mountain slopes of Spain's Picos de Europa, be prepared to pay for the privilege of having the right advice, guidance and legal protection.

At home we are used to paying fees to a solicitor, of forking out for stamp duty, and of paying surveyors for their inspections of the property. However unpleasant it is to pay these bills, we can at least guess what the fees will be to a fairly accurate level. With a property purchase overseas though, taxes, insurance and fees for professional services are almost universally more expensive and need to be budgeted for with accuracy. Do your research and take qualified advice.

Spain

More than 700 000 properties in Spain are owned by British families who clearly love the place. Most of these properties are second homes, used for private holidays and frequently rented out to others.

The main intention here is to walk you through the process of buying and selling a house or apartment in Spain. This is done right from the selection of the property to the point where you legally formalise the transaction, and includes a section on the procedures and processes necessary to give you protection and minimise the risks.

While the Spanish coastline has attracted huge development over the years, there is also an enormous amount to see and enjoy inland. When buying to rent your property, it is as well to consider who your tenants will be. On the coastal areas you will find holidaymakers seeking sunshine and seafood. If you have a remote property in the mountains of northern Spain, visitors are likely to be different and seeking a holiday experience that is about walking, climbing and wildlife photography, or privacy.

Just as in the section on buying holiday property investments in the UK, you should still be buying with an eye to your own use of the property. If this is not the case, consider the investment on commercial grounds where you will achieve the maximum number of rental weeks a year.

Even after the introduction of the euro, the cost of living in Spain is well below that of the Benelux and northern European countries. The weather is warmer and drier, and the variety of food and wines is tremendous. It is easy to travel to and the regions of the country are well-known, while all offering something unique in living opportunities as well as rental returns. The different coastal areas on the Mediterranean are the

Costa Blanca, Costa Brava, Costa del Sol. To the west is the island of Tenerife and to the east, in the Mediterranean, are the Balearic islands.

The biggest growth in developments of recent years has been the conversion of the Costa del Sol to its new identity as the Costa del Golf, so named for the courses along the 70-mile stretch of coastline from Gibraltar to Malaga. With the largest concentration of golfing facilities in Europe, golf courses have been accompanied by increasingly well-designed and built housing developments. Sotogrande and Rio Real are long-established estates and newer ones, such as the Santa Clara golf resort near Marbella, are fuelling the demand for good housing. Rental opportunities at such resorts are good for most of the year because the area appeals to general holidaymakers looking for good villa-based holidays, as much as to the sporting fraternity who want golf, tennis, riding, sailing, boating and watersports.

Inspection flights and property visits

An easy way to begin viewing Spanish property is to ring developers and join their inspection flights. These typically see you fly out to Spain for three days and give the opportunity to see several developments while also doing a small bit of sightseeing and dining on your own. The costs of these trips are low and usually include your return flight, travel to and from the hotel, and your meals.

Annie von Kirchner of Casa del Sol Properties suggests you give yourself the opportunity and the benefit of taking 'at least one inspection flight to each of the areas you are interested in. Ask the developers as many questions as you can from a check list written before hand. Stay as close as you can to the development you are considering investing in so as to get the truest picture possible of what the location offers.'

If you don't want to feel that you are being lead into making a decision and would rather sort out your own arrangements, please do so. The last thing you want is to come home with the title to a property you did not really want and to blame the purchase on having spent too much time in the company of enthusiastic sales people. All the good agents will be happy for you to make your own travel and accommodation arrangements to visit their sites, and can usually provide reduced rates for flights, accommodation and car hire.

Buying a place in the sun

Once you have identified the property you wish to buy and have agreed the terms and the method of payment with the vendor, you will pay a deposit to secure the property. At this point you create an 'option to purchase' contract.

At the signing of the contract the purchaser makes a proportional payment of the purchase price with the amount generally being agreed by both parties. For a one- or two-month option to purchase contract, a figure of 10 per cent of the purchase price would be usual. This amount is held as a trust deposit by the solicitor and handed over to the vendor when the title deed is signed. The date of the deed will be agreed in this contract as well as the conditions of the contract and the details of any consequences that arise in the event of failure to comply with the terms.

The option to purchase contract is a guarantee, both for the vendor, who is assured of selling the property, and for the buyer, who is assured of purchasing the property, all at the price established and agreed between the two parties.

The building contract   The building contract is a contract whereby one of the contracting parties, the contractor, is obligated before the other contracting party to carry out work at an agreed price. The last thing you want is an additional bill for an overrun. Ensure that you have a written confirmation from the builder in which they establish and confirm the time limits for completion of the work.

The price of the agreed work is generally paid when you take possession, but you can also opt for partial payments dependent upon the progress of the construction. In such cases you should again make sure you take professional advice to ensure the payment schedule is agreed in writing between both parties.

The cedula   The first occupancy certificate (cédula de habitabilidad) is issued once the work is declared to be complete. To obtain registration in the property register, you will need to make a declaration of new building before a notary. Expect to pay 0.5 per cent of the deed price to achieve this declaration.

The notary and the property register   All new properties in Spain, the rights and liabilities of same, as well as any changes to occur in ownership of the property, are registered in the property register. It is only the person whose name is recorded in the register as the titleholder who is able to transfer the title of the property. Given this, it is essential to verify and confirm that the vendor is the titleholder.

The notary is obliged to inform and verify to the buyer any charges or encumbrances (such as mortgages, embargoes and easements) that may be prejudicial on acquiring the property. This is achieved by the notary requesting a certificate from the registry office for the ten days before issuing the title deed, to establish that there has been no other request to register the same property.

The property is not immediately registered once the deed has been signed. The notary will make a preliminary entry that is done to prevent the registration of any other titles in respect of the same property during the 60 days it takes to process the final registration.

Expect the notary to charge between 1.5 per cent and 2.5 per cent of the purchase price for his or her fees.

Tax liabilities

Major builders with construction projects in Spanish housing and sport and leisure complexes have their own legal and contract teams of professionals. Between them they can advise you on all aspects of buying a house or apartment in Spain. Likewise, they will be in a position to advise you on tax law in respect of rental income on your property.

It will help if you can identify and understand the different taxes on buying and selling property in Spain and the percentage applicable in each case.

- IVA (Value Added Tax). In general, VAT is payable at 16 per cent.

- ITP (wealth transfer tax). Applied to all transfers providing they are not subject to VAT and is levied at 7 per cent of the deed price.

- A transaction will be liable to VAT or ITP but it will not incur both. Establishing whether a transaction is liable to VAT or ITP depends on whether the vendor is a person or a company. In any transaction where the vendor is a private individual the deal is always liable to ITP. Where the vendor is a Spanish company, it will always be liable to VAT except when it involves plots where building is not permitted.

- In the case of transactions involving foreign companies (offshore), these will be liable to ITP providing the companies concerned are not domiciled in Spain and therefore are not liable to IAE (business activities tax) or VAT.

- Plus valia (increase in value tax). This is a tax levied on the increase in value of the plot itself and serves as a local tax on urban property. The vendor is liable for its payment but it is negotiable and in practice is usually paid by the buyer. The amount varies according to the number of years the property has been owned. The level of tax is determined by the increase in the value of the land and the plot between the date of the previous deed and the current one. The local town council establishes the increase and determines the amount to be paid. The amount varies according to each individual case. Rural property is not liable to payment of 'plus valia'.

- IBI (property tax). This is a tax on property, frequently referred to as 'urban rates' and paid annually.

- Documented legal proceedings (stamp duty). The tax on 'documented legal proceedings' is included in the ITP, but is not included in VAT so a further 0.5 per cent is added to this tax. It is also applied to other forms of documentation such as your mortgage.

- Also, be aware of a payment on account which has to be made by a non-resident vendor of a property at the time the deed is signed. Where this is the case, the buyer has to retain 5 per cent of the deed price and pay it to the exchequer within a period of 30 days to account for capital gains. There is an exception to this. Where the property has been owned by the vendor (either a person or a company) for more than ten years, and has not undergone improvements, the 5 per cent retention is not applicable.

Even though common sense says there will be occasional changes, maintain contact with a professional adviser who will act on any financial and legislative changes.

Buyer's guarantees

It is important for you as buyer to take into account the following recommendations to obtain the best guarantees on buying a property:

- As the buyer you should verify that payment has been made for the latest IBI (property tax), as payment of this tax is the responsibility of the owner of the property.

- If your purchase involves an apartment liable to the payment of a community quota or contribution, you should verify that there are no outstanding payments.

- If it is a property that is not yet completed, the buyer should demand guarantees on any payments made on account. Do this through the use of a bank guarantee, trust account or special deposit account in the bank.

- Check to ensure that the municipal bye-laws permit construction of the property.

- If the property is new, check that it has the necessary installation papers to contract and connect electricity and gas supplies.

■ Check that the first occupancy certificate (cédula de habitabilidad) has been obtained.

Other financial obligations   You will need to nominate an individual or company (domiciled in Spain) to represent you before the taxation department as there are several annual taxes to be paid for owning a property in Spain. These are the wealth tax (IP) and the income tax (IRPF), and are paid by means of a declaration that you provide. In such cases, you should of course seek professional advice.

Foreigner's identity number   When you buy property in Spain, open a bank account, pay rates bill or buy insurance, you will need to have this awkwardly named number. It is easy to get from the nearest large police station to your property. This is a hangover from the years of old Spain, but will always be asked for in transactions with the authorities.

Residence status   Provided you are in the country and the islands for less than 183 days each year, you qualify as a non-resident. Where this is the case and you own a Spanish property you will:

■ have a fiscal representative;
■ declare your capital assets in Spain annually;
■ pay local rates;
■ pay income tax on your rental monies;
■ pay utility bills through your Spanish bank account.

Assessing the rental market

When you are looking to invest in rental units on the mainland or on the Balearics, consider the reasons that holidaymakers will be using your property and the local facilities they will be visiting. For example, will they be out sight seeing all day, returning only to change before rushing out again for the evening? Or are they going to spend the day around the pool, balancing their time between relaxing at the villa with trips out to restaurants? As an example of margins, consider that property in Mallorca will cost you twice as much as equally good property on the quieter island of Menorca, yet the rent is unlikely to be double.

If yours is simply a crashpad for young people determined to be out on the town all night, then keep it simple and find a reliable housekeeper or caretaker to keep an eye on the property and its contents. Where the holidaymakers are families booking for fortnightly stays and want childcare facilities nearby, then your options are more driven by making sure that the facilities in the property are of a high standard.

Where there is a mixed use of your property by people travelling out to Spain, not just to wind down and enjoy the weather, but to take part in particular hobbies, then the scope for longer periods of rental is higher.

David Vaughn of Sotogrande offers the suggestion that 'you can calculate the return on your investment over a longer than usual season where you have property at an established resort of mixed sporting and leisure use. When the June to August family holiday season is over you can enjoy several months of rental income from golfing and tennis-focused holidaymakers who will be visiting to improve their game when the UK weather can restrict this. From February until the summer holidays you can attract guests to your property who are taking short breaks and enjoying the leisure facilities, some staying for a couple of months at a time.'

Where there is a broad mix of facilities on a resort you can look forward to longer rental periods. Ocean View Property suggests looking at the potential for rental half of the year and keeping a few weeks or a month for yourself to enjoy the property. Based on pricing in 2002 on sites that offer good facilities for golf, boating and watersports, Fig.15.1 gives some numbers to consider when looking at the size or style of property.

However, not all properties will be new on large developments. You may prefer to buy your own place on its own plot. Whether you rent it out yourself or use the services of a letting agent there are some basics to take into account from the advice of Stan McHale who runs a property and villa maintenance business in Menorca:

- 'Anyone buying to rent on the island should ensure they work with a reliable property manager who has been in business for years. We find too many people setting up businesses and returning to the UK after a couple of years having not given it any commitment.

- Avoid having too many ornaments around your villa. Make it bright and welcoming to holidaymakers. You want them to enjoy themselves and return again.

- When you buy furniture, make sure the covers can be removed for cleaning after the season, because they are usually marked with sun tan cream and perspiration!

- Have the exterior of the villa painted every four years at least and the interior every two years. It is bad for your client to arrive at their holiday villa to find discolouring and paint flaking off the walls.

Figure 15.1   Rental income potential on a well-developed site

Income	Number of weeks	2-bed apartment (weekly)	3-bed apartment (weekly)	3-bed townhouse (weekly)	3-bed villa with pool (weekly)
High season					
(Late June – Sept.)	10	£650	£850	£1 250	£2 100
	Total	£6 500	£8 500	£12 500	£21 000
Mid season					
(Sept – Oct and					
Christmas and	15	£500	£650	£1 000	£1 600
New Year	Total	£7 500	£9 750	£15 000	£24 000
April – June)					
Low season					
(Nov – March)	10	£350	£450	£850	£1 250
	Total	£3 500	£4 500	£8 500	£12 500
Total rental	35	£17 500	£22 750	£36 000	£57 500
Expenses					
Management fee		£720	£800	£1 000	£1 500
(dependent upon development)		£700	£770	£850	£900
Cleaning and laundry bills		£720	£820	£920	£1 800
General service costs					
Total expenses		£2 140	£2 390	£2 770	£4 200
Net rental income		£15 360	£20 360	£33 230	£53 300
Purchase price		£108 000	£125 000	£165 000	£350 000
Annual return		14%	16%	20%	15%

■ We always meet our clients within 24 hours of their arrival and also on the day before they leave. This way any challenges can be put right early in their holiday or before the next tenants arrive.

Taxation of Spanish rental income

Even though you may not be resident in Spain for tax purposes, you will still need to make an annual income tax declaration.

The Spanish revenue authority is concerned only with the income you earn from your rental activities in Spain, as opposed to anywhere else. This would mean a tax on your rental property in Spain and on the interest on bank deposits held in Spain. While you obviously declare the same income on your UK tax return, you will get relief on the Spanish income provided it has been declared in Spain.

France

A good place to start when looking for a property in France, whether for the longer term as an investment or ultimately for your own home in retirement or relocation, is at one of the numerous property exhibitions. Vendors and agents will give you a reasonably easy opportunity to learn more about what property is on offer, the taxes and legal implications of buying in France, and a chance to meet others who have already made the decision to invest in French property.

Of course it would be foolish to make any decision based on a three-minute video, or one of the brochures that you will inevitably bring home. Instead, take an inspection flight and see for yourself the sorts of options that are open. Cheap flights to many regional French airports can get you to within about an hour's drive of most parts of the country.

A property finding agent will gently guide you through the requirements of your property in terms of space, age, style, grounds, number of bedrooms, facilities, local features and climate to come up with potential solutions to your quest.

Allow yourself three or four days in which to visit properties and also enough time to get a feel for the area when you are on your own, without the agent. The agent will take you through the purchase process and help find a solicitor to understand and complete the paperwork. Remember that once you have signed this contract you are committed to going through with it.

Getting hold of the mortgage funds is becoming easier and several UK banks now have French offices dedicated to financing investment property purchases. However, don't expect the process to take place at the speed you may be used to at home. Allow three months or so for all the papers to move from one party to the other and back again.

Purchase costs

When you come to buy a French property you can use a notary (a semi-public official) who will often act for both the buyer and the seller.

However, it is quite acceptable for the two parties to each be represented through their own individual notary but this role is not the same as that of a solicitor.

Purchase by an individual   The fees charged by the notary working for an individual will be charged on a sliding scale in line with the value of the property. The usual fee rate will be about 1 per cent of the purchase price. The buyer will also pay land registry fees and disbursements (also assessed on a sliding scale) at between 1 per cent and 2 per cent of the purchase price. As a result you can expect the total for legal fees to be between 2 per cent and 3 per cent of the purchase price.

Additional government purchase taxes will be payable if you are buying a property over five years old. These taxes are paid to the department or region and also to the commune and total a further 4.89 per cent of the price. If the property is new (less than five years old and being sold for the first time) there are no additional government purchase taxes to pay. Instead you have to pay TVA (VAT) and this will be included in the sales price.

Land for construction   If you are buying land with the intention of building on it, you may be better off by making the purchase in your own name as an individual. The alternative is to buy it in the name of the company but you will be liable for VAT at the normal rate of 19.6 per cent unless you qualify to pay it at the individual rate of 4.89 per cent. The advantage of buying the plot and then building is that taxes are levied on the value of the plot only. Usually the square footage will be indicated in your planning consent and fixed by the local planning authorities in accordance with local planning schemes.

There is an increased interest in self-build in France, not just with the expatriate community but with the French as well. Buying a plot or a *terrain* can give you the opportunity to design and build the house you want rather than try to buy a semi-derelict property and convert it. When you decide on a plot for building and it is not the *lotissements* or estates of modern design, where there will generally be one builder responsible for the construction of all the individual homes, there are other things to consider.

You may be buying a piece of private land that has come up for sale after a farming family no longer wish to work the land, or as a result of an estate duty sale where land is split up or sold off to raise funds. In this event, make sure that the plot is being sold as building land and has what is known as a CU (*certificate d'urbanisme*). This certificate will give you the peace of mind that the land is not in an area of flooding, that it is considered suitable for living on and, in general, is a piece of land where you can apply for outline planning permission.

Once you have the buildings plans and the sanction to build, where possible use a French builder as it will be noticed as a more positive move by your neighbours. However, this does not mean that French builders will make your life easy, especially when you learn that the French builder considers himself just that – a builder. He will not get involved in the electricity and plumbing arrangements and you will need to contract this to separate people. The whole process can be daunting and you will need specialist help that you will find locally.

Buying new property in apartments   New property in France carries a ten year guarantee much like the NHBC certificate in the UK. A deposit of 5 per cent of the purchase price will reserve your chosen apartment until the notary has drawn up the deed of sale documentation. When the notary signs this sales deed, you as the purchaser will be asked to pay part of the purchase price in proportion to the amount of work completed to date. This is in cases where the construction is not well advanced. Where the building has already seen a good rate of construction you will be asked to make staged payments in much the way you might expect to pay for a self-build or kit construction property. The usual payments for the construction of the apartment will be:

Foundations	35%
First floor	50%
Roof	70%
Watertight (windows, flashing, etc)	80%
Completion of the apartment	95%
Release of your keys	100%

Property taxes and service charges   When buying a property on its own, you will pay local taxes comprising the *taxe d'habitation* and the *taxes foncieres*. These are both levied in October or November and are based on the value of the property. The rates of tax charged are set by the region, the department and the local commune.

If you are buying an apartment within a block of holiday properties, perhaps in a ski resort in the Alps or the Pyrenees, service charges will usually include the caretaker and the communal heating as well as structural insurance. You will need to insure your own furniture and contents as well as paying for your own share of the utility bills within the property. In the case of the apartment block in a ski resort, you can perhaps find paid cleaning services through the buildings caretaker, contracting with them directly for this service.

Renting a French property

Throughout France you can find commercial letting agents able to take your property on to their books and let it for you. The most experienced companies can be recommended to you by other people in the rental and landlord community, though there are plenty to choose from. Expect to pay 20 per cent of the holiday letting income to the agents as their fee.

In the mountains and ski resorts, the practice of renting is probably the most organised with lets of a week or two weeks being common across the skiing season, while the owners may reserve a fortnight for themselves at a prearranged time. In the high altitude resorts, the winter season is obviously longer because of the temperature and the quality of the snow. Conversely, there is little or no summer season in a high altitude resort such as Val d'Isere; as a result you have no rental income for this time. Instead, you may wish to consider buying property in a dual-season resort where there is more activity available for a longer season. This gives you more tenants and better revenue.

When buying a property to rent to the ski audience you will do better to buy one that is close to the centre of a resort and preferably close to restaurants, bars and the ski lifts. Such locations will always rent faster and command better rental income. When looking at the size of ski property opt for two- and three-bedroom properties rather than one-bed and studio apartments. Individual chalets rent very well and it is less important for a chalet to be close to a centre or right on the piste provided they are attractive properties in their own right. Remember too that well-equipped chalets can command their most attractive rents for just a few weeks of the year.

Simon Malster of French Ski Properties offers some words of caution over the investment in chalet property, suggesting it is not for those with a shallow purse. 'Don't even touch it unless you are a committed and enthusiastic skier. A chalet is an expensive building lying empty for much of the year. The season in the high alps is a short one and if you are fortunate you will cover your insurance, your overheads and perhaps your mortgage payments from rental income. The money from rentals will allow you the chance to holiday in the alps without paying for a hotel, but on the whole don't expect a fast return. There are better things you can do with your money elsewhere in France.'

The estate agency process in France is very different from in the UK with only a few national agents. Branch networks are local and serve a region of the country. The market for lettings from the French community is different in that residential, as opposed to holiday tenants, will sign up for an agreement to rent that can be for as long as three years. It is virtually impossible for a landlord to get out of this once the document is signed.

Colin Trayte of French Discoveries helps UK buyers to locate and buy French properties and offers this suggestion about the different rental markets for cottage type property. 'Where the French take cottages or rural gîte holidays they expect a lesser standard of accommodation and facilities than do British holidaymakers. The French will use the property as a base for their summer holidays, which are usually taken only in July and August and be away for much of the day, returning in the evening. British holidaymakers want their cottage to be more of a home from home and stay close, enjoying the facilities of the property.'

In the south-west, Paul and Sarah Murray of Murray Properties have been running their business for several years providing a property management and holiday letting service for landlords. They find that most clients are UK-based landlords with one or two properties that they let as frequently as possible, saving a few weeks for close family at the same time each year. Many are considering a retirement to France and see the ownership of holiday property as the first step of the process.

Paul recommends that a landlord living in the UK 'should expect to pay 15 per cent of the weekly rent for a standard letting service where the property is marketed and advertised, security deposits and booking fees taken from the holidaymaker and rental payments are made to the landlord at the end of each month. For a higher level of letting service and tenant management, expect to pay 25 per cent of the weekly rentals.'

Dealing with other British nationals in the management and maintenance of your property can be a simple option for many and worth considering when you have looked at the properties you are considering for investment.

Paying tax

You need to declare income from rental activity to the French tax office by 30 April each year. Where income is greater than €15 000 a year, the taxpayer can elect to pay 30 per cent of gross receipts. You must consult with a tax official on the current accurate figure of income at which certain rates of taxation apply. Above this level, you can claim allowances for expenses such as management and letting fees, insurance, loan interest and depreciation of 1 per cent to 2 per cent of the purchase price. In this instance, net income is taxed at a minimum rate of 25 per cent. Where circumstances require you to pay French tax on your rental income you may claim credit for this against UK tax liabilities.

Mortgages

The use of mortgages in France is different from in the UK. It is fairly normal for banks to lend 80 per cent of the purchase price over a 15-year term. Interest rates in France tend to be lower than in the UK. Barclays and the Abbey National are both strong lenders on French properties via their subsidiary businesses.

There are various French banks with considerable experience of lending to British borrowers. These include BNP (Banque National de Paris), UCB (Union de Credit pour Le Batiment), Banque Transatlantique, Credit Agricole and Credit Lyonnais. Under French law, lenders cannot offer a mortgage where the repayments would be more than 30 per cent of the borrower's net monthly income (or combined income for joint applications). The 30 per cent figure includes any existing mortgage held in Britain. As a result of these criteria, it can sometimes be worth releasing equity on a UK property to support the French application with an increased deposit.

Inheritance and succession

Phillipe Pièdon-Lavaux of Blake Lapthorn cautions that inheritance laws in France, just as in several other European countries, can prevent a parent from disinheriting his or her children. Unless special arrangements have been made before the purchase of the property, the surviving spouse may have to share the inherited property with the children (even if they are from a previous marriage). These laws apply to a property in France even if the owner is normally resident outside France.

If you were to die without having made a will, your surviving spouse would be entitled to only part of the estate where there are surviving children. You can improve the position of the surviving spouse significantly by creating a will. To completely overcome these potential challenges of having only a limited claim to the estate (due to the existence of children from within the marriage or from a former relationship) you might consider the use of a tontine clause, the creation of a new French or UK company, or writing a marriage property clause.

It may be worth considering adopting a special matrimonial property regime called a *communaute universelle*. With the exception of some special situations, this would ensure the entire property passes to the surviving spouse without the payment of inheritance tax.

Capital gains tax (CGT)

Where capital gains tax is payable in France it may be offset against any UK liability, and as such you will not pay it twice. Partnerships, non-resident owners and companies (and this could still be a subsidiary of a UK-based company) will generally face a CGT liability of 33 per cent of the profit realised. However, against that liability you can claim for a variety of deductions. These include the costs involved in the original purchase, indexation to account for inflation and interest on loans that have not already been offset against rental income.

Italy

The buying process in Italy is a particularly regulated one where you should be certain of your decision to buy or to sell a property. Once the price has been agreed between the buyer and the seller each party signs a preliminary contract, described as a *compresso di vendita*. A deposit is paid amounting to a sum between 10 and 30 per cent of the sale price.

If the buyer pulls out of the deal, the deposit is forfeited. If the seller withdraws from the sale then twice the deposit value is repaid to the person who had wanted to buy. On completion of the sale, the balance of the purchase price together with all fees due are paid to the notary or *notaio*. The buyer and the seller each then sign *la scritura privata*, the document equivalent to the deeds of the property. Jenny Gale of Serimm Properties in Lucca explains that: 'The estate agent mediates the sale, with an equal commission taken from the vendor and the purchaser.'

> If the seller withdraws from the sale then twice the deposit value is repaid to the person who had wanted to buy.

Notary fees are likely to be 10 to 15 per cent of the purchase price and should be allowed for when considering the purchase. If you buy using an Italian mortgage you will also pay additional monies via your lawyer for having the charge levied by the lender registered with the land registry authority.

Expect to pay property tax or *imposta comunale surgli immobil* (ICI) at 0.4 to 0.7 per cent of the value of the property.

As with property elsewhere in Europe, it is important you work with a lawyer who will establish there are no unpaid debts associated with the property. Where these are found they can and should be separated from the property before you make the purchase.

If Europe seems too close and you hanker after more sunshine, look further west. Bermuda, Barbados, and the Bahamas offer a great deal of good property but have the added benefit that they attract affluent holidaymakers from both Europe and the Americas. To give you a flavour of the potential and the processes we look at the example of buying property on the island of Barbados.

Barbados

For a place that offers the convenience of access to the US, Latin America and Europe, Barbados is perfectly situated. Buying property here is far from cheap and yet the benefits are various. As a holiday destination a property here can earn good rental income and attract a variety of guests. It is also an ideal place to arrange six-month or one year rentals of your property given the relative shortage of good quality accommodation in response to the steady demand.

The government encourages foreign investment in island real estate through a number of useful policies, such as there being no restrictions preventing foreign nationals from buying and owning property. Also of attraction is the absence of estate duty or of capital gains tax on the sale of a property. Such welcoming policies have seen a growth of foreign investment, particularly in respect of the luxury market for villas and townhouses.

Transaction fees

Survey costs and sales commissions are borne by the vendor, and the 10 per cent property transfer tax was abolished in 1999. Each of the parties to a transaction bears their own legal fees, to a level between 1.5 and 2 per cent of the purchase price. The only other purchase cost would be the incidental costs of forming and then registering a company when a corporate structure is to be used for the purchase.

Upon selling the property, the vendor would usually incur: sales commissions of 5 per cent; stamp duty at 1 per cent; legal fees of about 1.5 per cent; and transfer tax of 10 per cent. On top of these, expect to pay annual operating tax of between 0.2 and 1.0 per cent of the property value.

Financing your Barbadian home

Most properties here are purchased with a mix of mortgage and personal finance. Local residents can buy on a 20 to 25-year mortgage option, but investors from outside can only take advantage of a 15-year term. Barclays Bank here will do mortgages for Barbadian property which is priced in US dollars. Expect to pay interest for your money at about 10 per cent, and for foreign currency loans to be done at about 3 per cent above LIBOR, the London Inter-Bank Offer Rate.

Other taxes   Once your property is on the short-term rental market, you will be required to apply 7.5 per cent VAT to the rental amount. Profit from rental activities is subject to income tax on the island. Where this money is earned through a company registered to do business in Barbados and where you are non-resident, the money sent back home to you (whether as dividend or interest) is also subject to withholding tax at 12 per cent.

The legal process

When you buy a house or villa in Barbados, once you and the other party have agreed on a price, the matter is handed over to lawyers. The vendor's attorney will draw up a purchase agreement which has then to be checked by your attorney. When you and the vendor have signed this document, you pay a deposit of 10 per cent of the purchase price. This moves from your attorney to the vendor's.

Until the deal is completed, the deposit is held in escrow. This changes as soon as the conveyance is agreed and the remaining monies are paid over. It is important when buying in Barbados to be able to show the funds came in from outside the island. Gain a central bank agreement to bring the funds into the island. Having achieved this, you will be able to show the introduction of funds from outside and earn the right to repatriation of monies realised. It may be stating the obvious, but this also means that it is illegal for a vendor to sell a property without the certificate of compliance that authenticates the origin of the money.

Paul Gregson of Knight Frank in London works with many landlords considering investing in overseas property from France to the Caribbean. His recommendation is that you 'buy your overseas property with either a very significant deposit of 50 per cent or more and that you even consider buying such property only with cash reserves. The opportunity to purchase expensive real estate in the more exotic parts of the world is greatly simplified if you can enter the market without the complication of arranging finance. When you do go ahead with an overseas investment, ensure you are protected by dealing with well-established firms acting for the seller and ensure that language is no barrier to good communication at all times during the purchase transaction.'

Developing your portfolio

irmingham Midshires, a specialist lender for property investment, made a survey of their borrowers in 2001. Of those surveyed, 64 per cent were looking to build a portfolio of between two and ten properties. Half of the respondents were buying to build additional security either for their retirement or financial future in general. Creating income now was a priority for 27 per cent of the respondents and 4 per cent saw the move towards investment property as a way to create financial strength for their children.

The likelihood is that as you buy a first and then perhaps a second investment property, your own ideas on the results you are seeking to achieve, will become clearer.

Don't be a 'trend' victim

The Council of Mortgage Lenders declared 2001 to be a record year for people taking out investment mortgages. By September that year more than £10 billion had been lent on more than 130 000 mortgages. But just because people think investing in property is a good thing is no reason for it to continue to be 'fashionable'. Many investors in property jumped on board as the value of their equity investments had fallen and at the same time as property prices climbed to high figures across the country. The result is that many landlords have ended up with a small portfolio of two or three houses where the borrowing covers just the mortgage repayments or where there is little equity in the property to be released when another good property comes onto the market.

It is likely that in the next couple of years many of those who bought property as an investment will sell out to reduce their exposure or because their friends are dumping property as well. It is difficult for a professional landlord to see this behaviour as anything other than irresponsible. It should not be possible to see yourself as a property investor and not consider yourself a landlord also when the two are so strongly linked. Where investors do dump property and move back into equities they are following a market movement and have probably missed the whole point of investing in the first place. Remember that property price trends will move up as well as down. We spoke at the beginning of this book about the importance of your deposit on a property buying an effective cash flow. If this is your major focus, it is unlikely you would hold properties for just a short time. In the short buy-and-sell scenario the tenant is seen merely as a convenient way to finance your hoped-for growth in property value before you can sell and reap the rewards.

When you buy a property and become responsible for its maintenance and upkeep, and for providing accommodation for your tenants, then the focus is on a long-term proposition. Expect to be a landlord for ten years or more and see your investments as being long-term ones. If you love property, you are unlikely to struggle with being a landlord, despite the difficulties and the challenges that come with the role.

Keep doing your homework

Continue to do as much research for property number four as you did for the first one. Stay close to local estate agents and also to mortgage lenders. Keep a watchful eye on the area where you are seeking to buy. Keep reading the local press for economic news and local politics as so much can affect your investment in an area.

Richard Donnell, Head of Residential Research at FPD Savills, in his 2002 survey of tenant demand cites that: 'Investors who focus more on the requirements of a wide range of occupiers will be best placed to take advantage of the opportunities and create above average returns.'

All too often investors buy flats and houses in areas where there is already overcapacity and the likelihood of a profitable rental went long ago. Seeing the scope for fast profits through perhaps buying outside your plan or in an area where housing can seem unbelievably cheap will often bring only headaches. Be on your guard against such things. When something appears too good to be true, there is often a reason!

Continue to be frugal

Under the right circumstance and after doing your research, buying to rent can be a significant decision in the development of your financial independence. Every penny you can save in your domestic or work environment is money that can be redirected to create cash flow for you and your family. Learn to stick with the savings habit and the discipline of investing for returns. It may be tempting to buy an investment house and see yourself with surplus income as a result. Instead, try to see the revenue from this property as being for you to recycle back into investment such that you make the money work harder to build cash flow.

It is human nature to want to treat yourself and spend the extra money, but if it is spent on other liabilities such as food, clothing, car finance payments, and credit card bills, it is not adding a penny to your financial security. The only way to find security is to set limits on what amount of revenue you will draw for yourself. If you spend £20 for every £100 you receive in rent and redirect the remaining £80 to buying more assets it will be a short time until you reach financial independence. At that point you will be very grateful you did not squander the early rental monies. Get your rental income to create more rental income.

Balance your investment

In developing a portfolio of property it is important to look at the make-up of your overall finances. When you first buy a property you may be doing it with the maximum loan possible against your earnings. As you buy a second and a third and then more properties it is useful to develop more balance so that you are protected in bad times as well as good.

Thomas Scrase, divisional director of Gerrard Ltd, the investment managers, recommends 'Buying to rent as a prudent adjunct to holding a mixed portfolio containing reserves of cash and some equities. Investment property deserves its place in a diversified portfolio of income-producing assets.'

Once you have a few well-managed properties, consider diverting some of the income into a cash reserve that can be of use when you need money quickly. This might be for an urgent need or to take advantage of an investment opportunity where financing procedures might prevent you from acting quickly.

Find your niche

As you learn the lessons of your first property and take the next step of getting a second and perhaps a third property, you are faced with an inevitable choice. 'Do I start to buy the same sort of properties all the time?' Not so difficult a question to answer, yet it does require some thought.

Do you prefer students to working people? What about tenants whose rent is paid from benefits received? Do you prefer busy working professionals who are short on time but able to pay the rent? According to your preference – and gut reaction is sometimes a true indicator – you should begin to collect property that supports your preference.

I love ex-council property and traditional terraced houses rented to people on average incomes and my focus is on profitable rental and regular cash flow.

Tony has always specialised in unemployed tenants whose rent is paid by housing benefit and who have tended to stay a long time in his flats. He would rather have this large stream of steady income, than lose a lot of time on his properties between short tenancies.

Amanda buys solid semi-detached properties and rents them to young, working couples. She looks for a mix of good rent and reasonable growth in the value of the properties.

Barry and Lou have a mixed portfolio of commercial shops and small offices, alongside their street houses which are generally rented to retired people. The offices and shops allow them to raise rent each year while the houses provide good cash flow and allow for the funding of other business ventures.

Philip buys flats in former industrial mills and renovates them before they are rented. The tenants are young people with decent incomes and no free time. They commute to work, but want to be just a short walk away from the social and leisure facilities of a town or city centre once they are home.

Others like to buy new flats on housing estates or developments just as the builders are releasing the plots for sale. If the estate is near a motorway junction and has been built by a certain developer, such people will buy these small houses and flats for rental to busy office workers.

Each of these examples is a choice and is driven by what the person enjoys from his or her investment strategy. Get the strategy right and work it consistently for the achievement of best results.

So what sort of portfolio do you want to develop? Figure 16.1 may help you focus on the essentials.

Future observations

A number of issues and situations can be expected to affect the growth of your portfolio business as a landlord. One of the more significant in terms of legislation is the introduction of the seller's information pack. This was intended for early 2003 but is likely to be delayed. This much-argued

Figure 16.1 What sort of portfolio do you want to develop?

1. My target income from rental cash flow is £ _____ a month

2. The type of property I want to focus on is _____

3. The average rent from such property is £ _____ per month

4. Therefore my financial goal is to own _____ properties at that rent

about product has been designed with the intention of speeding up the UK sales process by providing the buyer with quicker access to information about the property. Part of the pack will be a report on the condition of the premises, that in itself is useful and yet not a valuation. Even if it were to include a valuation, there would not be many who would trust a valuation from the vendor! It is possible the pack will contain a detailed homebuyer's report or survey, probably underwritten by insurance to protect the buyer from the cost of making good on any problems the surveyor had overlooked.

Other issues include the demographic ones that require you to think about the types of property you want to manage. The rise in divorce, the movement around the country to follow work and the growth in higher education all mean there is increasing demand for rented properties.

John Socha, Chairman of the excellent National Landlords Association comments that: 'The rise in divorce encourages short lets of up to six months while your tenant finds a decent property closer to their place of work, or near their children. The same statistic also affects the size of the properties that will rent well. There is little space in major cities and the value of a property is driven by the demand for land. What you can buy may command a high rent but the void periods can cripple you financially, especially if you buy at the top end of the market. The trend for what are known as microflats, a single-room with bathroom attached, is growing. Elsewhere, small one- and two-bedroom flats on larger development sites are being bought with great speed. The movement toward the work place and greater migration between jobs and flexibility of contract working is a further boost for the rental sector.'

As more students stay at university longer and achieve a further qualification, there is greater chance of them needing good accommodation close to the campus. However, if the number of mature students increases as people come to education after years at work, then their expectation of spacious accommodation will set new demands on the market. But landlords can meet such demands from more-affluent students who are bringing their savings into their education experience.

Each of these issues will have a bearing on whether you can succeed as a landlord. The significance lies in how you rise to meet the challenge of the changes.

Tax planning and portfolio development

To provide for their future long after their working careers have ended, many landlords want to link their properties with their pension planning arrangements. In short, they try to put their properties into a self-managed pension fund and are disappointed.

> To provide for their future many landlords want to link their properties with their pension planning.

The frustration comes from learning that residential property cannot be held as an investment within a property fund. Yet commercial property can be held in such a fund. Landlords should also consider that if they have created a pension fund, they cannot sell their own properties to the fund. If they could do so, the sale of a spare property might create a capital gains tax liability. Instead, it is worth considering taking rental income from the properties in your portfolio for as long as you live, reinforcing their use as a 'pension' source. At the death of the landlord, capital gains is not the issue, but inheritance tax is. The buildings within your portfolio can be placed in a trust to avoid them being classed as part of your estate.

Your solicitor and accountant can work with you on this aspect if it is appropriate.

Back to your strategy

Moving on to a more cheerful subject than estate planning, take time to review your strategy and the ways that this has been influenced by what you have read. If you were strictly a one-property person before going through the book have you changed to believe you can develop a multiple property portfolio? Where you may not have considered certain tenant groups, have you shifted your thinking? Perhaps you had never considered buying for the rate of return on investment before.

What matters is that you take the pointers that will bring you the greatest benefit and turn these into practical steps for the development of a portfolio and at the pace that is best for yourself.

Developing yourself

The power of association is great indeed. Yet it is a much-misunderstood behaviour. For whatever reason, our own experience of the world can sometimes prevent us from imagining that others with equal or greater experience would be willing to share information and wisdom. It certainly happened at school, that we learned from association with teachers. You may have been fortunate enough to have had a mentor in other areas of your life. So often, when you want to learn about a topic, the opportunity to associate with a good role model will present itself.

Where there are groups of landlords, housing associations, benefit officers and local council housing teams, you can learn a lot from spending time in their company. Opportunities for this present themselves often and you should consider taking advantage of them. At a local level, most towns and boroughs have a dedicated economic development team. Within either this group or the housing team of your council you will find someone who is responsible for working with and communicating policy to, the local landlords' forum. The name may vary from town to town, but the intention of such a group is the same – to provide private landlords with the chance to meet regularly, exchange views, and learn about issues that may affect their investments and their tenants. At the very least you will make good social contacts, and it is likely that potential opportunities will also come to you through this association.

I speak regularly to such groups as well as running our own Property Bootcamps and enjoy the opportunity to meet other speakers, landlords and like-minded individuals. Often you get the chance to learn about legislation from a local solicitor, to hear more about aspects of taxation that can affect your own profitability, or to discuss individuals self-tailored strategies. Typically hosted by the council, these events are usually free and provide you with a lot of benefit.

The magic of visualisation

As hinted at in the previous chapter, the benefits of knowing what you want are obvious. I would encourage you to take the time to visualise the beneficial outcome for your relationship or for your family of having your goals made real. Review the various exercises throughout the book. Look at the benefits you have decided upon and work hard with a property strategy that supports you.

Tony with his 20-plus properties remembers the day he bought the first one. 'I can see the moment as clearly as if it had just happened. I was getting on with my apprenticeship to be a butcher and I realised that after years of a career in a shop I would face my retired years with very little. That month I bought my first investment property and have repeated the process very regularly over the years.'

I wish you every luck with your buying to rent activities and decisions. Whatever you choose to do, I hope that you enjoy it. I would love to hear how you get on so email me on nick@buyingtorent.com.

LANDLORDS TALKING – RUTH

Ruth is an author and writing coach who has one investment property already and is considering another. The house is a three-bed terraced property bringing in a good monthly rent.

'The house we rent was our first. When we moved to another property we decided to keep the first one and rent it out. There is no mortgage on it and we manage the tenants ourselves without the use of an agent. I see the tenants at least four times a year to check on the property and see whether they need anything.'

'I can see us buying a further property as a form of passive income, allowing me to do the writing and coaching that I enjoy so much. On the next property a good cash flow will be important, but we would also want to see some capital growth.'

Appendix 1   Glossary

Advance   The money lent to you as a loan or a mortgage

Adverse credit   A poor credit rating or credit score

APR   Annual percentage rate. You see this in brackets after the main or headline rate for your mortgage. It includes costs other than interest rates, illustrating the true cost of your deal

Arrangement fee   The charge made by lenders for providing the loan to cover their costs

Arrears   Getting behind on your payment of the mortgage/any other loan

Assignment   The sale of a tenant's lease to another person

ASU   Accident, sickness and unemployment insurance, to cover the mortgage when you can't

Base rate   The rate of interest set by the Bank of England. Your mortgage lender may use this phrase when they describe their own standard variable rate or basic rate

Booking fee   A cost of reserving a mortgage rate, perhaps a special discount or fixed rate fee

Broker   A mortgage adviser who probably acts as introducer to a range of lenders

Buildings insurance   Protection in the event of damage to the structure of your property

Buildings survey   A detailed survey of a property

Buy-to-let mortgage   A loan against an investment property

Capital   The amount you borrow for the purchase of the property

Capped rate   The highest point to which an interest rate can go on your borrowing. A lender's variable rate applies only when it falls below the cap rate

Cashback   Money or a percentage of the amount borrowed that is offered to you once you complete on the mortgage

CAT-standard mortgage   A property loan that complies with and follows standards set out by government, with easy-to-understand terms and conditions, and transparent policies

Caveat emptor   'Buyer beware', a Latin phrase

CCJ   County court judgment. Issued because of an outstanding debt. Settle it quickly or it can go on your credit record and generally warns lenders off

Chattels   Any belongings that can be moved

Completion   The legal status of the purchase indicating the property is yours

Compulsory insurance   Insurance required by a lender as part of the contract

Contents insurance   Protection for the things inside your property and also for the things you regularly take out

Contract   Legally binding agreement signed by you and the seller, these are swapped or 'exchanged' to transfer ownership of the property

Conveyancing   Work done before exchange that involves the local land search, registering ownership with the Land Registry and the drawing up of the contract document

Co-ownership   Joint or multiple ownership of a property

Covenant   Part of the lease, this usually creates an undertaking between landlord and tenant as to behaviour that is or is not allowed

Credit check   Search done by a lender to gain access to financial records

Date of entry   Scotland. The date the buyer takes possession of the property

Deed   A legal document that is signed and delivered

Deposit   Sum of money paid to the vendor or seller on exchange of contracts to secure the purchase of the building

Direct mortgage   A property loan sold over the telephone

Disbursements   Solicitors' costs incurred in representing clients

Discharge fee   Charged by your lender once you have paid off the mortgage or before you transfer the borrowing to a new lender

Discounted rate   The rate fixed a certain percentage amount below the standard variable rate offered by your lender

Disposition   Scotland. The document that transfers title to the buyer

Early redemption   The penalty you pay to a lender for breaking out of their locked-in rate or for transferring to another lender

Endowment   A life insurance product that is an investment yielding enough to pay off the mortgage at the end of the borrowing period

Equity   The amount of the property you own, expressed as the valuation of the property minus the loan amount

Euro mortgage A mortgage for purchase of European mainland property and also available to those paid in euros

Exchange of contracts The moment that describes the swap of contracts between your solicitor and the vendor's solicitor

Factor Scotland. Professional property manager

Feu Scotland. Property that is for sale

Feuar Scotland. The owner of property

Feuing conditions Scotland. Conditions imposed by the owner of a house or a flat by the owner of the land under the property

Fixed rate A rate of interest fixed at a set level for a set time period

Fixed-term lease A lease granted on a property for a fixed period, measured in years

Fixtures Items fixed to the building that are included in a sale unless otherwise excluded

Flexible mortgage A mortgage with the opportunity to overpay or take a payment holiday

Flying freehold Freehold property built over another and not connected to the ground

Freehold Land ownership title

Freeholder Owner of the freehold. Can grant a lease of the property

Gazumping When a buyer is outbid by another, losing the property he was expecting to buy and also losing his costs to date

Gazundering Where the buyer drops out at the last moment

Ground rent Money paid by leaseholder to the freeholder

Guarantor The person who commits to being responsible for a loan in the event you can no longer pay it

Homebuyer's report A simple survey giving basic details of the property including a valuation and any obvious faults

Housing association An organisation operating on a non-profit basis with the aim of operating both rental and home-ownership programmes

IFA Independent financial adviser. An adviser who can recommend the best mortgage for your circumstances, not tied to a particular lender

Interest-only mortgage A mortgage where you pay only the interest, while saving the rest of the money to pay off the capital later

ISA Individual Savings Account. Usually for investing tax-free in equities, cash or life insurance; can also be used for an interest-only mortgage

Land Registry fee   Money payable to HM Land Registry to record the purchase or remortgage of a property

Lease   Document detailing the terms and conditions of the leasehold

Life insurance   Insurance paid out on the death of the policy holder or at a fixed term of years

Local authority search   Check done by your solicitor of local records to check for things such as subsidence, planning regulations or restrictions and possible changes in land use in the area

LTV   Loan to value. The amount expressed as a percentage that the lender is willing to lend against the property value

Maisonette   A flat over two stories in a larger block

Management company   Company set up by group of tenants in a block or by landlord to manage a property and deal with repairs and maintenance

Memorandum of sale   Written summary of the terms and conditions of the sale. Sent to seller, buyer and solicitors once the sale is agreed

Microflat   A purpose designed living space in a city where cooking, TV, eating, and sleeping activities take place in one room

MIG   Mortgage indemnity guarantee. Insurance necessary where there is less than 10 per cent equity in a property and where you are asking the lender to increase their risk

Missives   Scotland. Exchange of contracts

Mortgage   A loan secured on property

Mortgage deeds   A legal document that describes the terms of the mortgage and the interested parties

Mortgagee   The provider of the finance, e.g. a bank or building society

Mortgagor   The borrower of the loan

MPPI   Mortgage payment protection insurance. A policy to pay the mortgage in the event of your inability to service the mortgage due to loss of work or sickness

Negative equity   Your property is worth less than you borrowed to buy it

New-build   Newly built property

NHBC scheme   A national building guarantee on newly constructed property

Non-status loan   Loan agreed without an in-depth search of your financial details, may be useful if you are recently self-employed

Notary   French official involved in property transfer process

Notice to complete   This is served by either the buyer or the seller via their solicitor in the event of a delay to completion on the previously agreed date. If the delay was your fault and you do not complete there will be fines or a loss of deposit, etc.

Off-plan   Buying a property before the development has started

Open market value   The price the building will fetch where willing buyer meets the demands of the seller

Pay rate   The interest rate payable on the mortgage

Pension mortgage   An interest-only mortgage. Repayment monies go into a personal pension with tax-free benefits leaving, hopefully, enough to pay off the outstanding monies at the end of the term

Portable   A mortgage that you can transfer and take with you when you move house

Premium   Your regular contribution to pay for life or other insurance

Probate sale   Sale of a property after the death of the owner

Purpose-built flat   A flat that was built as a group of similar flats, usually with a common entrance

Quotation   Supplied by a possible lender, this contains all aspects of the costs of borrowing with them

Reddendum   The aspect of the lease that details the ground rent payable and the timetable for payment

Redemption   Making a partial or a total repayment of your mortgage

Remortgaging   Borrowing against the equity in a property, either with the existing lender or a new lender

Rent-to-mortgage   Scheme by which council tenants can have rent payments allowed as contributions toward eventual purchase of their property

Repayment mortgage   With this mortgage, repayments cover the interest while also repaying some of the capital borrowed

Repayment vehicle   The repayment of an interest-only mortgage

Right to buy   Scheme that allows council tenants to purchase their home

Search   Request for information, made by your solicitor or yourself to the local authority, or the Mines record agency or Land Registry

Self-certification   Declaration of earnings to a lender, perhaps supported by an accountant, but usually accepted with little further checking

Service charge   Money paid to the landlord or to the management company of the property for services provided to tenants

Shared equity   Method of buying in partnership with a builder who provides an interest-free loan or deferred repayment

Shared ownership   Buying with a housing association

Sitting tenant   Person has the legal right to remain in the property, even when sold to a new owner. Useful with some investment properties

Sole occupancy   Declaration of status of occupancy to a lender that means you will have no tenants in this property with you

Stamp duty   Government tax levied on properties with a value over £60 000

Standard construction   Brick-built house with tile or slate roof

Studio flat   A single-room home, with separate WC and possibly a separate kitchen

Subject to contract   This is the time between the sale being agreed and before completion of contracts. Vendor or buyer can still back out with no comeback

Sum assured   The payout value of an insurance policy

Tenant   The person with their name on the lease, also known as the lessee

Term assurance   A form of life assurance providing cover within a specified time in years. Beyond this there is no life cover

Title deeds   The documents that provide legal ownership to a property

Tracker rate   Loan with an interest rate that follows an established base rate

TVA   French version of VAT

Upset price   Scotland. The property price above which you must bid

Vacant possession   The previous occupants must move out before you can move in

Valuation   Inspection by a qualified surveyor acting for the lender to ensure the value is in line with, or greater than, the amount being borrowed

Variable rate   A rate of interest fixed by lenders, different from the Bank of England base rate but still in line with it

Vendor   The seller

Appendix 2 Websites and contacts

Association of British Insurers   020 7600 3333   www.abi.org.uk

Association of Residential Letting Agents   01923-896555
     www.arla.co.uk

British Association of Removers   020 8861 3331   www.bar.co.uk

Department for Education and the Environment   www.dfee.gov.uk

Derbyshire Country Cottages   01629-583545
     www.derbyshirecountrycottages.co.uk

Council for Licensed Conveyancers   01245 349599   www.theclc.gov.uk

Council of Mortgage Lenders   020 7437 0075   www.cml.org.uk

Council for Registered Gas Installers   01256 372200
     www.corgi-gas.co.uk

Federation of Overseas Property Developers, Agents and Consultants

     020 8941 5588   www.fopdac.com

Gerrard Limited   01865-243581   www.gerrard.com

Health & Safety Executive gas safety advice line   0800 300363
     www.hse.gov.uk

HM Land Registry   020 7917 8888   www.landreg.gov.uk

Housing Corporation   020 7393 2000   www.housingcorp.gov.uk

Howsons Accountants   01538 393600   www.howsons.co.uk

Independent Financial Advisors Promotion   0117 971 1177
     www.ifap.org.uk

Independent Housing Ombudsman Limited   020 7379 1754
     www.ihos.org.uk

Independent Schools Information   www.isis.org.uk

Inland Revenue stamp duty helpline   0845 603 0135
     www.inlandrevenue.gov.uk

Land Registry valuations   www.landreg.gov.uk

Lane Fox Banbury   01295-277161   www.lanefox.co.uk

Law Society   0870 606 2500   www.lawsociety.org.uk

Law Society of Northern Ireland   028 90 231 614   www.lawsoc-ni.org

Law Society of Scotland   0131 226 7411   www.lawscot.org.uk

Local Councils and Poll Tax   www.local.dtlr.gov.uk

Local Government Association   www.lganet.gov.uk

Mortgage Professionals, The   0870 233 152   www.mortgagepros.co.uk

National Association of Estate Agents   01926 496 800
www.naea.co.uk

National Federation of Residential Landlords   01202-686868
  www.nfrl.org.uk

National House-Building Council   0870-241 4302   www.nhbc.co.uk

National Inspection Council for Electrical Installation Contracting (NICEIC)
  020 7564 2323   www.niceic.org.uk

National Landlords Association   0870 241 0471   www.landlords.org.uk

Office of the Banking Ombudsman   020 7404 9944   www.obo.org.uk

Office of the Building Societies Ombudsman   020 7931 0044
  www.financial-ombudsman.org.uk

Office of Fair Trading   020 7211 8000   www.oft.gov.uk

Office for the Supervision of Solicitors   01926 820 082
  www.lawsociety.org.uk

Postcode searching of areas   www.upmystreet.co.uk

Property Auction News   01709 820033

Registers of Scotland   0131 200 3940   www.ros.gov.uk

Relocation agents   www.relocationagents.com

Royal Institution of Chartered Surveyors   020 7222 7000
  www.rics.org.uk

Scottish Homes   0131 313 0044   www.scot-homes.gov.uk

Street Maps   www.streetmap.co.uk

Total Trade Services   0800 0851531   www.totaltrade.biz

Area search websites

www.upmystreet.com   Great for knowing what is near to that auction
  property in a town you don't know

www.hometrack.co.uk   Gives a good assessment of the value of
  properties in a specific area

www.ukpropertyguide.co.uk   Introduction to property sites and provision of local information by postcode

www.london.gov.uk   Source of all information on the Greater London Authority, including development plans

www.environment-agency.gov.uk   Check out pollution levels, flood warnings, safety hazards by postcode

Property search websites

www.assertahome.co.uk   Great site with good postcode and price search

www.ukpropertychannel.com   Busy site featuring listings of more than 2000 estate agents so you get loads of local information about a community or an area

www.estateagents.co.uk   Helpful site with information and advice on topics from borrowing on a mortgage to tips on renting out property

www.primelocation.co.uk   Great for pricey property in trendy areas but no good if you want high yields from traditional rental markets

www.move.co.uk   Easy site to navigate with good advice on the process of buying and moving and simple postcode search

www.rightmove.co.uk   Popular site that gives you an option to store a portfolio of favourite properties

www.newhomesnetwork.co.uk   A good site if you are looking for modern properties for renting to a professional tenant group. Good site with the ability to search for developments countrywide

www.findaproperty.com   If you want something unique and special you are more likely to find it here, as well as property news and good links to overseas property websites

www.fish4homes.co.uk   Classified advertising site with content driven by newspaper style advertising format and access to property searches by area and postcode

www.thisislondon.co.uk   Based on Evening Standard newspaper. Search for all manner and price range of London property. Can give you a good confirmation of what rentals can be achieved by postcode

www.properties-direct.com   Listings for many of the professional businesses such as solicitors, lenders, and packing firms, as well as the standard property search facility

www.yell.com   Broad-based search for business ad services listings and also a strong property section www.propertyfinder.co.uk   Search for higher value properties here, with links to agents and their letting and management departments

Auction companies

Allsop & Co.   (Residential) London   020 7494 3686   (Commercial) London   020 7437 6977   www.allsop.co.uk

Andrews & Robertson   London   020 7703 2662   www.a-r.co.uk

Athawes Son and Co. London   020 8992 0056
www.athawesauctioneers.co.uk

Austerberry   Stoke-on-Trent   01782 594595   www.austerberry.co.uk

Bigwood   Birmingham   0121 456 2200
www.bigwoodassociates.co.uk

Butters John Bee   Stoke-on-Trent   01782 261511
www.buttersjohnbee.com

Caxtons   Maidstone   01622 609050   www.caxtonsauctions.co.uk

Cottons   Birmingham   0121 247 2233   www.cottons.co.uk

Darlows   Newport   01633 250485   www.tmxdarlows.com

Dedman   Southend-On-Sea   01702 311010   www.dedman.net

Drivers & Norris   North London   020 7607 5001   www.drivers.co.uk

Edwin Evans   London   020 7228 5864
www.edwinevansproperty.co.uk

Handleys   Leeds   0113 246 9090   www.handleys-leeds.co.uk

Mark Jenkinson   Sheffield   0114 276 0151
www.markjenkinson.co.uk

Leonards   Hull   01482 375212   www.leonards-hull.co.uk

Main & Main   Cheadle, Cheshire   0161 491 6666
www.mainandmain.co.uk

Miller Metcalf   Bolton   01204 535 353   www.mmauction.co.uk

Keith Pattinson   Newcastle-upon-Tyne   0191 213 0550
www.pattinson.co.uk

Seel & Co   Cardiff   02920 342721   www.rhseel.co.uk

Sherry Fitzgerald   Dublin   00 353 1 661 6198   www.sherryfitz.ie

Shonki Brothers   Leicester   0116 254 3373   www.shonkibrothers.com

Strettons   London   020 8520 8383   www.strettons.co.uk

Suffolks   Ipswich   01473 210200   www.suffolks.co.uk

SVA Property   Edinburgh   0131 624 6640   www.sva-auctions.co.uk

Weaving & Partners   Liverpool   0151 708 8484   www.weaving.co.uk

Wilsons   Belfast   02890 342626   www.wilsons-auctions.com

Winkworths   London   020 8649 7255   www.winkworths.co.uk

Overseas property

Abbey National France   00 33 (0)3 20 181 818   www.abbey-national.fr

Accord Immobilier Sales & Rental   00 33 (0)4 68 119 696
   www.accord-immobilier.com

A Place in France   02392 832949   www.aplaceinfrance.co.uk

Allez France   00 33 (0)5 49 270 122   www.allez-france.com

All France Properties   020 8891 1750   www.all-france-properties.com

Alpine Apartments Agency   01544 388234

Blake Lapthorn Solicitors   020 7430 1709   www.blakelapthorn.co.uk

Building Design Consultancy France   01722 333583
   www.adrian-barrett.co.uk

Casa del Sol Properties   01243-379797   www.casadelsol.co.uk

Charente Property   00 33 (0)5 45 854 993
   www.charenteproperty.co.uk

Cornish & Co Solicitors, Spain   0800 163507   www.cornishco.com

David Dale Removals   01423 324948

Eden Villas, Spain   01382-505101   www.edenvillas.co.uk

English in Provence   00 33 (0)4 90 742 354
   www.englishinprovence.com

European Property   www.europropertynet.com

Fox Hayes Solicitors   0113 209 8922   www.foxhayes.com

FPD Savills   020 7408 5520   www.fpdsavills.co.uk

French Discoveries   0121 449 1155   www.french-discoveries.com

French Property   01702 390382   www.french-property.com

French Property News   020 8543 3113
   www.french-property-news.com

French Real Estate   00 33 (0)4 97 030 333
   www.french-property-search.com

French Ski Property   020 8905 5511   www.frenchskiproperty.com

Hamptons International   020 7493 8787   www.hamptons-int.com

Homefinder   00 33 (0)5 55 710 781   www.homefinder.50megs.com

Ian Stewart Architect   00 33 (0)4 78 300 192   www.architect.fr

King & Co Spanish Mortgages   01489-578888

Knight Frank   020 7629 8171   www.knightfrank.com

Leisure & Land   020 8951 5155   www.leisureandland.co.uk

Links French Property Services   01525 519411
    www.links-property.com

Live Languedoc   00 33 (0)4 68 456 962   www.livelanguedoc.com

Stan McHale Property Management Menorca   00 34 971 368 879

Maison Minders Letting Agency   00 33 (0)5 65 246 646
    E-mail: maisonminders@aol.com

Murray Properties France   00 33 (0)5 63 339 511
    www.murraypropertiesfrance.com

Ocean Estates, Spain   0800 328 0444   www.ocean-estates.com

Ocean View Property   0121 693 0170
    www.oceanviewpropertiesonline.com

Pannell, Kerr, Foster (Guernsey)   01481 727927

Richman-Ring Removals   01795-427151   www.richman-ring.com

Riddell Croft & Co. Solicitors   01473 384870   www.riddellcroft.com

Scott Dunn Ski   020 8767 0202

Serimm Properties, Lucca, Italy   0039 0583 467450   www.serimm.net

Simmonds en France solicitors   01425 653355   www.enfrance.co.uk

Spanish Homes magazine   020 8469 4384
    www.spanishhomesmagazine.com

Spanish Property for retirement   www.spanishpropertyco.com

Sotogrande UK   020 7736 1700   www.sotogrande.com

Tarn Properties   00 33 (0)5 63 572 632   www.tarnproperties.co.uk

VEF French Properties   00 33 (0)2 96 134 000   www.vefuk.com

Viva Estates Spain   020 7436 9500   www.vivaestates.com

White & Company Removals   01252 541674